THE BONDS OF DEBT

THE ENIGMA OF CAPITAL

THE BONDS OF DEBT

RICHARD DIENST

VERSO
London • New York

This edition first published by Verso 2011
© Richard Dienst 2011

1 3 5 7 9 10 8 6 4 2

Verso
UK: 6 Meard Street, London W1F 0EG
US: 20 Jay Street, Suite 1010, Brooklyn, NY 11201
www.versobooks.com

Verso is the imprint of New Left Books

ISBN-13: 978-1-84467-691-0

British Library Cataloguing in Publication Data
A catalogue record for this book is available from the British Library

Library of Congress Cataloging-in-Publication Data
A catalog record for this book is available from the Library of Congress

Typeset in Minion Pro by Hewer Text UK Ltd, Edinburgh
Printed in the US by Maple Vail

Contents

Acknowledgments

I am grateful to the friends who helped me write this book: Vince Leitch, Bruce Robbins, John McClure, Richard E. Miller, Susan Willis, Henry Schwarz, Saree Makdisi, Cesare Casarino, Patricia Clough, Ross Dawson, Ramsey Eric Ramsey, Diane Gruber, Stephen Pluháček, Heidi Bostic, and Jeremy Glick. Thanks to Aleksey Kasavin for making the index. I would also like to thank Reynolds Smith and two anonymous readers, who read the whole manuscript and offered excellent feedback. I've been fortunate to be able to discuss this work with audiences in many places (including several times at Rutgers and the CUNY Graduate Center), and I thank all the organizers and audiences for their engagement. Many thanks to Sebastian Budgen, Mark Martin, Jane Halsey, and everyone at Verso.

For her help in writing, not-writing, and everything else, I cannot thank Karin enough.

I am especially grateful for the generosity of my teachers: the late Masao Miyoshi, who got me started, and Fredric Jameson, who kept me going. I dedicate the book to them.

Introduction: All That We Owe

Who will write the history of these troubled times? For many years now we have heard one overriding story, the official story, rehearsed day by day before global audiences. By its reckoning, the inexorable forces of capitalism are remaking the world once and for all, their victory ensured three times over—by the allure of their wares, the threat of their arms, and the blessedness of their cause. Every setback or sign of resistance has been portrayed as one more reason to finish the job. In the wake of a tumultuous twentieth century and in the face of mounting uncertainty, the self-proclaimed victors of history keep declaring that there is really only one zeitgeist blowing us along: the spirit of total commerce, pitched at the most encompassing level possible, capable of bringing everything to market and bringing the market to everyone. As long as the economic prescriptions are followed, any kind of political system can join the cause, so-called dictatorships and so-called democracies, strong states, weak states, and failed states. No time for losers: the recalcitrants and reprobates simply have to join up, drop out, or be left behind. From now on, the newly rehabilitated angel of history promises nothing but good news to those who heed its call—or so we are told, incessantly, even when there is nothing but bad news to tell.

The official story was never true, but it remains powerful. Although their victories have never been as decisive as those of ancient generals and golden-age imperialists, the rulers of our era do exercise a special kind of dominion. Above and beyond the monopoly of violence claimed by the major states, there has emerged a new kind of command, a monopoly of actuality, exercised on one hand through the power of teletechnology to shape the world in its own image, and on the other by the power of money to decide what deserves to exist.[1] The effective horizon of this control oscillates somewhere between the news cycle and the business cycle; moment by moment it translates everything it knows into the present tense. It seeks its glory not only in ratifying its mastery over what happens today; it meticulously amortizes what used to be and assiduously discounts what is yet to come. The past is worth saving only if it is worth saving right now, and the future, insofar as it has not already been paved over or scheduled for expiration, will just have to take care of itself. Cut loose by destabilizing flows of capital and caught by ever tighter nets of competition, people everywhere live more fraught, more bewildered, more defensive, more pressured lives. Market ideology, working its way deeper into the textures of social life, becomes something more absolute: a legitimation of every present indignity for the sake of unnamed opportunities to come. Market logic, elevated to the status of a natural law, demands that everybody should live within the circle of free choices and calculable consequences, even while inventing a full range of techniques to deprive nearly everyone of effective freedoms, channeling rewards immediately upward while dumping bad consequences onto those least able to bear them, somewhere else and sometime later. Through the vigilant management of expectations and the peremptory refusal of alternatives, our common life is split up into countless schemes for survival.

So while the spirit of our age still celebrates military strength and technological invention—if only because warfare and high technology are still crowned with the highest spiritual justifications—the

---

1   Jacques Derrida has written of the "monopolization of actuality" in his interview/essay, "Artifactualités," in Derrida and Bernard Stiegler's *Échographies: de la télévision* (Paris: Galilée, 1996). Although the exact phrase does not appear there, the phenomenon had already been analyzed throughout the work of Guy Debord.

main historical plot is being written in the prolific and obscure scripts of capital. That is why the official version of this history will not be written by "the victors" but by the creditors, for whom every human accomplishment or aspiration becomes subject to henceforth interminable wrangling and hoarding. In a world where basic decisions about everything from fisheries and crop rotations to pharmaceuticals, nuclear power, and old-age pensions are ruled by extraterritorial economic reason, the most basic circuits of social life—alliances, obligations, and solidarities—have been hotwired to disseminate corrosively antisocial energies. Any expression of collective possibility and promise, beleaguered in the best of times, must struggle to make itself heard in an atmosphere filled with endless chattering in praise of immense wealth.

In a moment like this, the most fateful world-historical figures are not captains of industry or globetrotting entrepreneurs, let alone heads of state, but central bankers, fund managers, insurance brokers, and the legions of traders and fixers swarming behind them. They do not presume to rule this world by themselves, trusting in their own righteousness; each wants merely to carve out the most profitable niche, manage one or two variables, guess the trends, beat the averages, take a cut, charge a fee, and let the rest of the world go its way. They do not care for policy or planning, except where it might jack up or bite into their profits. They are generally indifferent, even ignorant, about the global system they help to animate. Their sense of history is calibrated by the split seconds of arbitrage, the volatile turnover of portfolios, the slipstreams of interest, the fitful jockeying over exchange rates, and the implacable arithmetic of the actuarial tables. In striking their deals and hedging their bets, they aspire to achieve a kind of bootstrap transcendence, suspended for as long as possible between "too soon" and "too late," long enough to seize a good chance but not long enough to face the fallout or the blowback. Nobody who can wield the power of capital wants to be stuck in the stubborn temporality of material things and everyday life, even if that remains the only world there is.

The so-called "financialization" of the global economy encompasses more than the operations of financial capital. More to the point, it implies the networked reorganization of all economic activity, an omnilateral overdetermination of all local and sectoral markets, each one with every other. The integrated, instantaneous transmission of "market signals" tends to make every transaction ever more subject to transnational variables beyond recognition or control, inflected by everything from exchange rates and credit costs to subsidy patterns and commodity futures. Only the most powerful players can deploy their interests across these disparate and differential time zones: decisive competitive advantages are secured by those who have the means to maneuver capital from one economic stratum to another, especially through abstract instruments invented by the latest financial technologies, keeping one step ahead of their fiercer rivals and two steps ahead of the rather less fierce regulators. In staking their positions, the financial swarm appear to be interested only in playing the margins and leveraging their stakes, treating anything in their path as an infinitely fungible mass of value to be broken up, reconfigured, and played off against itself. To find the smallest edge, traders stay glued to their screens, appraising every piece of news for chances and dangers, sifting torrents of information for glimpses of intuition or premonitions of fate. The first draft of history—the only one that matters to them—scrolls across the screen with the divine serenity of raw data, abbreviated in the ciphers of rates and prices. Everything else is mere commentary.

In order to appear natural, necessary, and inevitable, market institutions have always called upon both scientific discourse and showbiz hucksterism. But now the circuitries of economic exchange and electronic media are becoming ever more closely fused: each echoes the other, blending the solemn voice of certainty with the yapping and howling of animal spirits. While the markets look to the media for clues about what to do next, the media look to the markets for clues about the meaning of what just happened. This sloppy feedback loop instills quick decision-making reflexes and permanent uncertainty at the same stroke. The market-media machine, created over the years as much by political default as design, has become a global organ of countergovernance, and it will continue to mutate whenever its functional autonomy is threatened by regulation or supervision. Not only does its expansion reframe the temporalities of investment and the uneven development between sectors and regions, it also creates its own apparatus of enforcement, whereby the mood swings and stubborn grudges of market discipline become the most decisive kind of reality. Heeding its mixed signals, the planners, bureaucrats, and managers set their watches and pretend to be in charge. Everybody else is supposed to keep working, obey the local authorities, enjoy the show, and wait patiently for a lucky break. Such is the historical role global capital wants to assign to the vast majority of the world's population, for now.

For now. But if this diagnosis holds true, it would be hard to see how the future could offer anything other than more of the same, and more and more of it, punctuated by breakdowns and marginal reforms, outliving all of us until the planet is exhausted. That is why so many attitudes and opinions about our epoch in its state of crisis, no matter how varied they may seem when lined up on the shelf, typically do no more than consecrate the general insecurity and confirm the inertia of foregone conclusions. By cornering the resources of memory and anticipation alike, the current order of things lays claim to all the time in the world, a world perpetually in debt to the power of what already exists.

The chapters in this book approach the current situation through the question of indebtedness. It is a partial and roundabout approach, stemming at least in part from the way the concept of indebtedness itself keeps shifting from economics to philosophy, from psychology to sociology to anthropology and elsewhere. Even these disciplinary markers do not really touch upon what we already think we know about debt. It seems obvious that everybody lives in a state of indebtedness, yet people sometimes speak as if it were a state that can and should be avoided, as if debt were something we could simply do without. At the same time, people tend to take the need for indebtedness for granted, striking a bargain moment by moment between the force of circumstances and the way things ought to be. One way or another we try to shape our own debts into a personal footprint, a mixture of wanting and waiting, of having and giving up.

That is why it seems a mistake to try to pin down either the concept or the experience of indebtedness in a single definition. It is certainly true that credit card companies rely upon vague feelings of guilt to collect their bills, and that contemporary nations impose financial obligations upon all of their members in the name of individual freedom—but it seems impossible to decide where practical calculations end and moral imperatives begin, just as it seems impossible to say where a sense of autonomy and self-sufficiency stops and a recognition of the needs of others begins. Instead of opting for one disciplinary language over another, it seems better to trace the outlines of the question in several different ways, in various theoretical idioms and using rather different objects of analysis. All of which is to say that these essays, taken together, try to engage with various discourses on indebtedness, different nodes or clusters where thinking about the state of the world cannot help but examine the ways we do or do not feel bound to it. Indeed every discourse on indebtedness proposes a certain notion of the "we," and no matter who that "we" might be—and precisely because it might change from one moment to the next—we owe it to ourselves to learn which debts are worth keeping and which ones are not.

1 Once in a Lifetime

At first nobody knew what to call it. Everybody agreed that a "crisis" had broken out, but then again there is always a crisis going on somewhere, and this one seemed different. The stock markets were sliding, central banks were scrambling, and politicians were trying to figure out how to take sides against a looming disaster that would engulf them all. The media mouthpieces, having no idea what was going on, began to speak in tongues: brokers' stoicism, bankers' self-pity, and populist rage all at once. As the mood darkened and the experts began to tussle over which dire scenario was unfolding, it became clear that a recession was already going on. The next step had to be at least a "slump," probably a "crash," and maybe a "depression," but there were lurking doubts as to whether even those labels went far enough. All at once the "credit crunch" and the "financial freeze" became a "tsunami" and a "meltdown," as if only a deadly natural catastrophe or a nuclear disaster could be an adequate metaphor for what now gripped the global markets. (Recall that "tsunami" was Alan Greenspan's choice, while the IMF opted for "meltdown.") The apocalyptic rhetoric, springing from the mouths of revered oracles, had the desired effect: everybody got scared. Bailouts were rammed through, emergency powers were invoked, and a few well-paid heads rolled. Then, as soon as the first burst of panic died down, the rewriting began.

It did not take long before a crowd of explanations, interpretations, and predictions started wrangling over the story line. The upheaval had been clearly centered in the US financial sector, but as hindsight led further and further backward, the source of the troubles became ever more diffuse and the scale of the problems grew. In the first revisionist narrative, the whole mess became the "subprime mortgage" crisis, as the wrathful finger of blame singled out the untold legions of deadbeat homeowners who were failing to keep up with their house payments, thereby upsetting the banks' careful calculations. Outrageous stories were circulated detailing the presumptuous and reckless efforts of people with very little income to buy expensive real estate. A moment later it was decided that there must have been something wrong with the federal government's efforts to help poorer people buy homes, because such people were obviously not ready for the solemn duties of property ownership. That story had to be revised when it emerged that those subprime mortgages had been processed en masse, like factory-farmed cattle, into innocent-looking and highly rated securities which, like fast food hamburgers, could no longer be traced to any particular source. Although the weakness of the mortgages could be estimated, the value of the securities suddenly seemed completely unknowable. It turns out that many kinds of financial transactions work that way, churned out by what is now known as the "shadow banking system," through which a full range of arcane and now rather insecure securities had been bought, sold, and scattered across balance sheets and portfolios large and small. For a short time the complexities of the shadow banking system seemed to offer some kind of key to the perplexing situation, a secret logic or a hidden agenda, although nobody seemed to know how it really worked. Most commentators professed to be shocked and dismayed that things had gotten so far out of hand, although the complaints were usually followed by a grudging admission that the only people who could clean up the mess were the very same people who had created it. Likewise, the ratings agencies and accountants who had been signing off on the dubious valuations were now enlisted to assess the damage and design the rescue. As the troubles continued and the explanations were recycled and refined, it became clear that there was plenty of blame to go around. Sooner or later it would be everybody's fault, because everybody had been lulled by easy credit and rising markets. And so it was nobody's fault, since nobody could have seen this coming, and even if they had, any effort to stop it would have violated the core principles upon which the whole system is built.

Just as liquidity problems turned into solvency problems, so a localized crisis of confidence turned into a systemic crisis of knowledge. It unfolded in several stages over the course of 2007 and 2008, reaching its most intense phase in mid-September 2008. According to the theory of efficient markets, uncertainty and risk always go hand in hand, so reluctant buyers should be able to demand a discount, driving down the prices of the more dubious deals. When traders begin to decide that they do not know enough about the securities they are trading, prices are supposed to drop, the issuance of new securities is supposed to slow, and there should be more insurance and hedging all around. Even with a sudden cool-off, the system can sputter along until confidence returns. But when there is enough skepticism stalking the markets, uncertainty cannot find its price. Any asset can become toxic once the market freezes up, not simply losing value but effectively counting for nothing at all. Likewise, a loan can go irretrievably bad anywhere along the line, whether through the failure of the lender, the borrower, or any of the long line of intermediaries between them. The autumn of 2008 brought more than that: the very fact that the financial system had seized up at all proved traumatic. The so-called risk management models, which were advertised as techniques for dealing with imperfect information and providing protection from supposedly less likely scenarios, simply fell apart under the waves of doubt. The best proof that there really is a global capitalist system has been provided not by its successes but by its failures: its markets are most efficient when they are transmitting fear.

As financial institutions of all sizes scrambled to determine their exposure to these abyssal risks, it became clear to everybody that both internal and external oversight of the industry had been disastrously negligent or ignorant or both. Esoteric debates over accounting rules broke into public view because many institutions simply clammed up, refusing to set a value on their losses, to pay out on insured claims, or to take massive write-downs. Banks stopped lending to each other, swindles unraveled, hedge funds vanished, once-mighty behemoths shrank to shadows of their former selves, whereupon they were gobbled up or turned into wards of the state. Hardly anybody objected to the emergency lines of credit and other concessions offered by the Federal Reserve, but the debates sharpened as liquidity injections turned into equity stakes, and federal authorities imposed conditions that were not entirely welcome to those who were being saved from ruin. (Wall Street firms thus replayed a scenario from imperial military history: having "invited" the United States government to intervene, they were shocked to see the troops setting up permanent bases.) If all the big players can be paid off without debauching the currency—an outcome that is still uncertain—the financial system will be handed back to the private sector in fighting shape, although it may henceforth have to operate under new guidelines devised by their once and future colleagues sitting in the administration. Yet it is hard to escape the impression that the debates over re-regulation have been halfhearted: all of the participants were united in their effort to "save capitalism," and one way or another huge sums of public money found their way into the hands of multinational banks, insurance companies, and individual investors. Despite a full round of confessions and accusations—a duet between mea culpa and I-told-you-so—nobody in the public eye seems to have stopped believing for a second that this thing called capitalism can and should rule the world.

What the various stories and interpretations have in common is the impression that there has been a day of reckoning, a moment of truth, a time when old illusions dropped away and the real state of affairs was at last revealed. Each version positioned the turning point in a different place and drew rather different conclusions. If the troubles had been brewing for just a few months, or a year or so, there would be no need to undertake any fundamental rethinking: it was just a cyclical shift that got out of hand, so perhaps shuffling the leaders in Washington and Wall Street was enough to make sure it does not happen next time. Taking a slightly longer view, the current difficulties could be blamed on the convergence of bad luck, greed, and incompetence that accompanied the reign of George W. Bush, perhaps enabled by the Clinton-era deregulation of banking: now that Bernanke, Summers, Geithner, and the other children of Greenspan have learned from their mistakes, the regulatory regime can be patched up again. But as soon as one begins to trace the problems any further back in history, the major trends of the recent past will begin to seem unsound and a whole epoch will be called into question.

The turning point might be sought about thirty or thirty-five years ago, that is to say, somewhere in the mid to late 1970s, when an Anglo-American blend of neoconservative politics and neoliberal economics gained ascendancy and unbridled capitalist globalization took off. Whatever historical basis there may be for this periodization—and we will examine some evidence shortly—it has the polemical advantage of treating the current crisis as a moment of truth for a whole passage of world history, up until now dominated by the triumph of the market model, the emergence of the US as the sole superpower, and the emergence of China as the biggest new engine of wealth creation and accumulation. Seen in that light, the present conjuncture would be more momentous than that of 1989, which now appears to have merely confirmed global tendencies already under way. (The tanks in Tiananmen Square and the fall of the Berlin Wall would now signify the same process: the implacable advance of market culture, whether enforced at gunpoint or imposed by default.) Likewise the current juncture would have to be considered more decisive than 1968, another monumental date that now seems to be nothing more than the high-water mark of an era that has finally washed away. Indeed, precisely because the past thirty years can be seen as a prolongation of a whole postwar trajectory (and thus a repudiation of its countercultural and antisystemic movements), the present turmoil could be delivering a judgment on the past sixty years or more. Such moments of closure, along with the sense of renewal that follows, are supposed to come only once in a lifetime.

There is one problem with this attractive story: the moment of truth never happened. There has been no transformative revelation, no collective coming-to-our-senses, no realignment with reality, no *Vergangenheitsbewältigung* for the boomer generation. The passage from unhinged cries of panic to the restoration of confidence has been rather smooth, even while trillions of dollars of paper wealth were disappearing. The crisis of knowledge—as messy, confusing, and embarrassing as it was—did not turn into a crisis of faith. Capitalism could be declared saved from the brink of disaster precisely because its partisans and guardians cried out for a rescue without ever admitting any mortal danger. The media presented the whole ordeal from the Roadrunner's perspective rather than the Coyote's: the Roadrunner knows that if you run off a cliff, you won't plummet as long as you never look down. Nevertheless, there may be some adjustment in the rhetoric from now on. There might even be a new kind of compromise within established opinion: the free market fundamentalists no longer need to claim infallibility in order to get what they want, while the idealists and the skeptics can finally give up on the idea that there is any alternative to the present system. In that sense, this moment may indeed have been a once-in-a-lifetime event, an ideological somersault in place, led by those who want us to believe in capitalism more than ever.

It will not be easy to keep the faith. Both the media-driven panic (short-lived) and the ideological turmoil (quickly calmed) obscure a more fundamental and permanent kind of crisis, one that makes it just as impossible to start over as to carry on as before. We will call this situation a *crisis of indebtedness*, operating in at least two dimensions. In the first place, the present crisis can be understood as a debt crisis in the classic sense, the piling up of unserviceable obligations, the leveraging of values beyond belief, and a breakdown in the mechanisms that maintain credit and more generally the capital form of value itself. In a broader and more elusive sense, this is a crisis in the social and psychic relations that make economic debts possible: the various forms of economic belonging, selfhood, responsibility, and mobilization that make indebtedness of any kind durable and binding. As different kinds of debts stack up, more than ever people find themselves too much bound to everything that exists. This is not only a problem with everything that exists—the whole world brought to order by a juggernaut system that requires so much energy, time, and space just to keep going—but it is also a problem with the way we bind ourselves to it, and to each other. It is hard to imagine that this more fundamental crisis will be over anytime soon.

It will be necessary to tell the history of the present differently. The readily available narratives have been exhausted and the new ones have not yet projected their horizons very far. In order to get a sense of what stories it might be possible to tell, we should begin with a comparison of several critics of contemporary capitalism who share a common virtue: they understand how the system works without taking for granted that it will survive. At the same time, as opposed to the critics and skeptics who are always predicting disaster, in their work they concentrate precisely on the capacity of the system to profit from its imbalances and to stave off collapse a little longer. Although everybody seems to agree that the financial crisis signaled the end of something, and perhaps even the end of many things at once, it is even more important to examine how and why everything else keeps going.

Robert Brenner

Robert Brenner presents a theoretically sophisticated and empirically detailed analysis of the global economy in his two books, *The Economics of Global Turbulence* (1998/2006) and *The Boom and the Bubble: The US in the World Economy* (2002). Brenner's basic narrative is divided into two parts: an account of the "long upturn," which lasted from the late 1940s until 1973, and then, in sharper focus, an account of the "long downturn" that has persisted ever since. There are three main protagonists in his story: the United States, Germany, and Japan—or to be more exact, the combined business and political elites of these countries, insofar as they act in concert for their mutual interests. Brenner does not tell the protagonists' stories the way they like them to be told, each centered on itself, but as the tectonic shifting of overlapping zones, in which the external relationships between them prove more decisive than their own internal dynamics. As the (unsigned) preface of the 1998 edition puts it:

> Here it is not the vertical relationship between labour and capital that in the last resort decides the fate of modern economies, but the horizontal relationship between capital and capital. It is the logic of competition, not class struggle, that rules the deeper rhythms of growth or recession.[1]

At every step, Brenner notes, the narrative is driven by the "*unplanned, uncoordinated, and competitive* nature of capitalist production*,*" where individual agents and national strategies, acting with what might seem to be impeccable business sense, nevertheless drive the system into dead ends over and over again.[2] The world

---

1   Robert Brenner, "The Economics of Global Turbulence," *New Left Review* I:229, May/June 1998, p. iii.

2   Robert Brenner, *The Economics of Global Turbulence: The Advanced Capitalist Economies from Long Boom to Long Downturn, 1945–2005*, (London: Verso, 2006), p. 7 (emphasis in original). Henceforth abbreviated EGT.

economy, here represented by its fiercest regional leaders, goes through several rounds of success and revenge, where the supposedly benign search for comparative advantages turns into an implacable threat of mutually assured destruction of wealth. During the long upturn, the United States managed to secure the lion's share of rewards from the rapidly growing world economy, both by prolonging the wartime boom of its domestic economy and by organizing the postwar global trading system to its advantage. Germany and Japan played catch-up by pursuing more statist varieties of capitalism, geared toward poaching shares of world trade from the US and the UK.[3] The growth pattern reached its limits by 1973, which Brenner attributes largely to "international manufacturing over-capacity and over-production."[4] Throughout the long downturn, this problem does not go away, and the rest of the story concerns the fitful and misguided attempts by the various economic agents to break out of the downward-dragging spiral. Brenner wants to explain not only why the downturn happened, but also why it has persisted.

His interpretation is presented in three parts, each of which demarcates both a phase in a process and a level in a structure. The first moment or level he describes as the "anarchy and competitiveness of capitalist production," in which each capitalist pursues his or her own interests without regard for the needs of the system. "As long as everything goes well," Marx wrote, "competition acts . . . as a practical freemasonry of the capitalist class."[5] Evidently this kind of competition, supported in some fashion by the state, provided the updraft during the 1950s and 1960s. But as soon as "chronic overproduction and overcapacity" sets in, competition becomes, in Marx's words, "a struggle of enemy brothers."[6] As profits are squeezed, each

3   EGT, p. xxi.

4   *Ibid*, p. 141.

5   Karl Marx, *Capital*, Volume Three, trans. David Fernbach, (London, New York: Penguin, 1981), p. 361.

6   *Ibid*, p. 362.

competitor must either take a loss and get out, or look for cheaper ways to stay in the game, thereby forcing others to do the same. At this level, one might expect conventional economic theory to declare that all is well: once there has been sufficient exit from the scene, accompanied by the destruction of whatever capital was sunk in the failed enterprises, the survivors stand a chance to regain higher profitability. But the very persistence of the long downturn, with its numerous false dawns and overhyped booms, suggests that there will be no easy path back up.

At the second level, Brenner lays out a different kind of obstacle to the recovery of profits: the fact that investment and exit do not happen continuously and smoothly, but rather in "waves, or blocs, of interrelated placements of fixed capital."[7] This jagged pattern characterizes "uneven development" in Brenner's use of the term: the gaps between "early-developing" and "later-developing" blocs of capital constitute a new axis of competition. Older and newer ensembles of capital, more or less entrenched in different kinds of investment, battle over diminished opportunities to turn a decent profit. Thus, to take one example, the technology bubble of the 1990s grew so huge precisely because it seemed to herald a new wave of greater profitability (grounded in greater productivity across all kinds of sectors), in the process rendering a great deal of older fixed capital redundant. In Brenner's account, however, the tech boom should be seen as only one component of the equity bubble of the late 1990s. That glorious surge was driven not by the advent of a new technological wave but rather by the codependent irrationality of markets intoxicated by the prospect of endless short-run returns and a Federal Reserve confident that it could make everybody feel wealthier (due to rising stock and real estate prices) without ensuring that some kind of underlying wealth was actually being produced. The whole episode demonstrates, in terms of the larger argument, how efforts to break free

---

7   EGT, p. xxi.

from the constraints of overproduction and overcapacity have so far ended up prolonging the decline by extending the lifespan of older chunks of capital.

But, as Brenner demonstrates, the double whammy of anarchic competition and uneven development operates on yet a third level: the long-range maneuvering between the US, Germany, and Japan to find a national or regional strategy to overcome the downturn that all three have propelled. Instead of providing leverage to allow each to break free from the others, competition ensured that they would all share a similar fate within "an advanced capitalist world that, *as a whole*, remained fettered by reduced profitability and mired in quasi-stagnation, evincing ever-decreasing vitality, business cycle by business cycle, between 1973 and 1995."[8] As overall growth stalled, each protagonist sought some formula, combining trade policy and currency revaluations, to break the cycle of lower profits, investments, outputs, and productivity. Nowhere did the brief phases of recovery ever reach the heights last seen in the 1960s, and from the vantage point of 2006, Brenner concluded that all efforts had failed across the board. Again we have to ask: Why?

At each stage of the story, the economic field becomes more crowded: too many capitalists, too much machinery, too many commodities, too much mobile capital. "What makes the new century's bubbles and imbalances potentially so lethal is that they have so far covered up and compensated for serious underlying weakness in the real economy."[9] In falling short of the profitability demanded by its owners, the sheer weight of all the capital produced in recent decades can be kept aloft only by circulating more paper claims on future expectations:

---

8   EGT, p. 280 (emphasis in original). Nicholas Crafts has objected to this claim in detail in "Profits of Doom?" *New Left Review* 54, November–December 2008, pp. 49–60.

9   *Ibid*, p. 336.

[We are witnessing] the still further continuation of the long down-turn against a background of over-supplied lines of production, decelerating aggregate demand, and a mountain of over-priced paper assets, *all made possible by the accumulation of private and public debt at unprecedented speed and at historic levels.*[10]

It is important to stress that Brenner does not treat this financial expansion as a cause of the prolonged downturn, except insofar as it disguises or blocks the reckoning that ought to come. Indeed the buildup of debts cannot help but drag more and more sectors of the system into crisis, even where corporations have tried to "mend their balance sheets" and the bubbles inflated by easy credit have been more or less rudely popped.[11] From such a perspective, there is nothing to foresee but ever more constricted stagnation and greater turbulence, if not a more cataclysmic breakdown.[12] Shorn of its Promethean glamour and its Utopian underpinnings, capitalism reaches the end of this tale broken, helpless, and disoriented.

---

10   EGT, p. xxiii (emphasis added).

11   Robert Brenner, *The Boom and the Bubble: The US in the World Economy* (London: Verso, 2003), 302. The 2003 Postscript outlines the consequences of easy credit at the turn of the millennium in the form of three bubbles in the US economy waiting to pop: overpriced stocks, inflated house prices, and a massive current account deficit. He summarizes the situation as a

self-undermining process in which the inexorable rise of US obligations to the rest of the world enables the rest of the world to grow through exports at the expense of US productive power and therefore of the capacity of the US to honor those obligations . . . opening the way to rising interest rates, falling asset prices, and a plummeting dollar that would undercut a US and global recovery. In the middle of 2002, Alan Greenspan announced that the recession was over. But the economy is still far from out of the woods. (pp. 311–12.)

Even after the crisis of 2007–2008, the bubbles still have some air in them, and nobody is saying anything about getting out of the woods.

12   EGT, p. 343. For Brenner's own account of the crisis, see "What's Good for Goldman Sachs Is Good for America: The Origins of the Present Crisis," available at: escholarship.org/uc/item/0sg0782h.

Giovanni Arrighi

Giovanni Arrighi tells an equally startling but very different kind of story. In *The Long Twentieth Century* (1994) and *Adam Smith in Beijing* (2007), along with smaller texts and collaborative works, he offers a grand-scale recasting of the historical and geographical evolution of capitalism since the fifteenth century. Arrighi insists that he did not set out to construct such a massive edifice: he began with the slightly more modest intention of examining the "long twentieth century" of US ascendancy, stretching from the 1870s to the end of the 1990s. But Arrighi also wanted to show how the trajectory of US ascendancy reiterated the patterns of earlier "long centuries" of expansion. In order to tell that story, he found it necessary to elaborate a more general theory of the world system itself, based on the conjunction between economic "systemic cycles of accumulation" and political hegemonies oriented by "territorialist" imperatives. The history of the system takes its shape from the ways these distinct and otherwise divergent forms of power are reconciled, for a while, before giving way to a new geography of capital with a new governing center. On one hand, Arrighi finds, there have been four systemic cycles of accumulation, the Genoese, Dutch, British, and American. On the other hand, there emerged three successive state formations capable of exercising a world hegemony, centered first on the uneasy leadership of the Dutch, and then on the more unilateral power of the British and the Americans. Thus his narrative aligns and contrasts the trajectory of US power in the long twentieth century with the "long nineteenth century" of the British and the "long seventeenth century" of the Dutch. (Curiously enough, the eighteenth century, usually cited as the cradle of the industrial and democratic revolutions that gave birth to modern capitalism, loses its pride of place in this chronology.) It is already clear in the 1994 book that Arrighi expected that a major realignment of global power was already under way, although it was not clear whether

Japan could pull it off; by 2007 the only question was how quickly the relocation of the global epicenter to China would take place, and with what degree of disruption and violence.

In the present context, the most striking component of Arrighi's project is his account of the inner dynamism of the "systemic cycle of accumulation" that gives each of the long centuries a similar shape. First comes a "material expansion" under the aegis of a dominant bloc powerful enough to control interstate competition and "ensure material cooperation."[13] Then, as the productive potentials of such an arrangement reach their limits, a "financial expansion" takes off, as capital increasingly abandons the hazards of material production in pursuit of more liquid, more speculative returns. For Arrighi, this alternation of material and financial expansions, anchored by a hegemonic center, accounts for the emergence of capitalism itself, yet as each cycle concentrates a greater degree of power, it also hastens its own exhaustion. The beginning of the financial expansion can be seen as the "signal crisis" of each cycle, but it may be some years before a "terminal crisis" marks the point of no return.

From this perspective the whole period since the early 1970s (Brenner's "long downturn") appears not only as the desperate search for profitability but also as the twilight of US hegemony. Over those years, the US sought to deploy its military and financial powers to secure what advantages it could: spreading the neoliberal gospel of free trade, whether using the soft or hard option, became the only way to make the most of a losing hand. Superior firepower working together with the privileges of the almighty dollar gave the US the capacity to run an ever mounting current account imbalance with the rest of the world. It is often observed that the US since the 1980s went from being a creditor nation to being the world's biggest debtor: this was no accident at all, but rather the most plausible strategy, as

---

13   Giovanni Arrighi, *The Long Twentieth Century* (London: Verso, 1994), p. 12.

more and more global capital abandoned material expansion and indeed "development" itself.[14]

Arrighi's emphasis on the cycles of expansion builds upon the arguments advanced by Fernand Braudel in his three-volume study of capitalism and civilization in the fifteenth to eighteenth centuries. Braudel's work, however, famously evades the strictures of conventional historical narrative; instead, his account maps a capitalist civilization structured on three levels. The lowest of these levels is "material life," people living within the parameters of self-sufficiency and survival, largely unaware of the systems and flows that surround them. In the middle is a "market economy," functioning as the ordinary circuitry of exchange relationships extending in ever larger and denser networks. At the top is capitalism proper, an accumulation of financial power that both grounds itself in the labors of material life and rises above the traditional markets.

Indeed, Braudel insists that capitalism should be understood as an "anti-market" sphere, unfolding at the "very summit of society." He traces the origins of modernity to the mounting power of the early financiers and their growing attachment to the state, achieving the optimum formula only in the mid-nineteenth century, "when the banks grabbed up everything, both industry and merchandise, and when the economy in general was strong enough to support this edifice permanently."[15] In Arrighi's view, the ascendancy of capitalism over the market economy is not permanent or irreversible, and the tension between them has returned with a vengeance in the current situation. He wants us to entertain the possibility that the present terminal crisis might not lead to yet another systemic cycle,

---

14 The now classic argument that neoliberalism constitutes nothing less than an abandonment of modernization itself is presented in Robert Kurz, *Der Kollaps der Modernisierung* (Leipzig: Reclam Verlag, 1994). Perhaps China would be the exception that proves the rule.

15 Fernand Braudel, *Afterthoughts on Material Civilization and Capitalism*, trans. Patricia M. Ranum (Baltimore and London: Johns Hopkins University Press, 1977), pp. 62–3.

once again guided from the commanding heights of capital, destined for hegemonic domination and financial apotheosis. Instead, the decades ahead might bring a historically original kind of market economy, in defiance of what has seemed like a natural life cycle embedded in capitalist modernity.

In *Adam Smith in Beijing*, Arrighi traces the emerging contours of an especially vigorous material expansion with Chinese characteristics. The terminal crisis of the US systemic cycle has exhausted the Western "capital-intensive, energy-consuming" path of accumulation, which had been in force since the takeoff of the British cycle (circa 1820). Now an Eastern "labor-intensive, energy-saving" path is taking the lead, boosted by Western technologies selectively adapted to its needs.[16] The ascent of East Asian economies may be impressive but it is not uncritically celebrated: Arrighi notes these economies' growing inequalities and offers a guarded assessment of their longer-term prospects, especially given their ecological recklessness. The more speculative question for Arrighi is whether China's path might, in an unexpected and belated twist, realize Adam Smith's vision of market-led growth, shorn of the upper-level concentration of power that characterizes the capitalist mode of production. Such a prospect would not only strip market logic of its transcendental force, it might also provide a rather different role for the state than the one granted in the neoliberal dispensation, where the state must scramble as a competitor for capital on the global markets, following strict policy prescriptions in order to attract capital from potential creditors. Rather than serving as conduits of fiscal discipline under the tutelage of Washington, political institutions pursuing this alternative path might take on unaccustomed tasks, such as reorienting policies "towards a more balanced development between rural and urban areas, between regions, and between economy and society." Indeed Arrighi holds out hope that China's ascent might "contribute

---

16 Giovanni Arrighi, *Adam Smith in Beijing: Lineages of the Twenty-First Century* (London: Verso, 2007), pp. 37–9. Henceforth ASB.

decisively to the emergence of a commonwealth of civilizations truly respectful of cultural differences."[17] Within the vast horizon of Arrighi's text this hopeful prospect is not yet a prophecy, and there remain plenty of countervailing currents as well as counter-arguments. (Among other objections, one might note Slavoj Žižek's warnings about a coming era of "authoritarian capitalism," taking Lee Kuan Yew of Singapore as its founding father.[18]) But Arrighi's argument, pitched on the broadest plausible historical scale, offers an unexpectedly optimistic and open-ended glimpse beyond the apparent closure of the present moment.

David Harvey

David Harvey's recent work, especially in his books *The New Imperialism* (2003) and *A Brief History of Neoliberalism* (2005), approaches the present conjuncture through the geographies of uneven development and the dynamics of class power. His analysis complements Arrighi's, exploring the dynamic relations between the logics of accumulation and the exercise of territorial power, although we can also set Harvey's description of the victorious, well-nigh messianic celebration of free-market orthodoxy alongside Brenner's picture of capitalists struggling to regain lost levels of profit. It is no accident that the intellectual arrogance and relentless boosterism of neoliberals has been accompanied by a mediocre and lopsided economic performance. (In the United States, this aura of success has been a notable achievement, generating not only a numbing political consensus but also enlisting significant personal investment to prop up the markets.) By emphasizing the institutional victories of neoliberalism—whether inflected by neoconservative or "third way" rhetoric—Harvey poses questions that do not figure in Brenner's or Arrighi's work, in particular questions that

---

17   ASB, p. 389.
18   Slavoj Žižek, "Berlusconi in Tehran," *London Review of Books*, July 23, 2009, p. 3.

concern the ideological and political conditions that have accompanied the current system. How indeed could an apparently marginal and strictly academic theory have come to rewrite the basic operating rules for the entire global economy? Here is Harvey's initial description of the phenomenon:

> Neoliberalism is in the first instance a theory of political economic practices that proposes that human well-being can best be advanced by liberating individual entrepreneurial freedoms and skills within an institutional framework characterized by strong private property rights, free markets, and free trade.[19]

As he goes on to explain, such a conception is loaded with assumptions about "human well-being" and "freedom" that demand a leap of faith. By taking "free enterprise" as the ideal instance of human freedom, neoliberal policy celebrates and rewards those powers that only the wealthy can wield, while disguising the fact that that kind of freedom is not meant to be shared and thus that the advancement of "human well-being" was never the goal after all. In wrenching the notion of freedom away from the various strands of post-sixties culture, neoliberalism established itself as a "market-based populist culture of differentiated consumerism and individual libertarianism."[20] It proved to be a potent formula in the US and the UK, where it was presented as the antidote to visibly failing institutions and disappointed hopes.

Apart from its ideological zeal, the neoliberal round of accumulation acquires its specific force through a comprehensive arsenal of economic, political, and legal techniques that Harvey calls "accumulation by dispossession." Under this heading he designates both old and new forms of coercion and expropriation, comprising everything

---

19   David Harvey, *A Brief History of Neoliberalism* (Oxford: Oxford University Press, 2005), p. 2. Henceforth BHN.

20   *Ibid*, p. 42.

from the various forms of "primitive accumulation" described by Marx (whereby land, labor, and natural resources are turned into commodities) to newer processes including biopiracy, privatization of publicly owned assets (including the nationalized property of former socialist states), and the exploitation of cultural, collaborative, and intellectual labor. Neoliberal states become key agents of dispossession by learning to manipulate social and economic turmoil to carry out redistributions of wealth at home and abroad.[21] Thus Harvey stresses that the credit system itself functions as a "radical means" of dispossession: the "strong wave of financialization that set in after 1973" has created deeper forms of debt peonage, spectacular forms of fraud, and expanded opportunities for legalized corruption and market manipulation.[22] All of these techniques tap into new zones of value in an attempt to evade the obstacles posed by an economy already choked with unprofitable investments, obsolete fixed capital, and mobile surpluses.

Accumulation by dispossession, then, provokes a new range of antagonisms and struggles running along the internal and external borders of the capitalist system. In some instances, these struggles signal new possibilities for radical politics, but Harvey is keen to emphasize that the older lines of contestation over "the expansion of wage labour in industry and agriculture" remain in force.[23] The analysis presents a political dilemma: on one hand, the full-spectrum strategy of neoliberalism faces resistance on many fronts at once. On the other hand, amid the profusion of struggles and the variety of their rhetorics, every project of resistance runs the risk of losing sight of the fact that the system of capitalism itself remains the main opponent. As Harvey puts it, borrowing a flourish from Ronald Reagan, "The first lesson we must learn, therefore, is that

---

21 David Harvey, *The New Imperialism* (Oxford: Oxford University Press, 2003), pp. 144–8. Henceforth NI. See also the summary in BHN, pp. 160–5.

22 NI, pp. 147, 156.

23 BHN, p. 178.

if it looks like class struggle and acts like class war then we have to name it unashamedly for what it is."[24] And so Harvey's first reading of the crisis of 2008 was an unashamedly class-based one: coming after the neoliberal restructuring of the state and the financialization of everything, the bailout of the banks and insurance companies was tantamount to a "financial coup against the government and the people of the US," consistent with the past three decades of policies aimed at consolidating the capitalist class, especially its financial wing.[25] Whatever world-historical logics may have been playing themselves out in the crisis, the response of the Bush and Obama administrations has demonstrated that the champions of the current order are not about to admit defeat.

The regime of indebtedness

To readers of Brenner, Arrighi, and Harvey, the financial tumult of 2007–2008 could not have come as a surprise, and would have been immediately recognized as a symptom of bigger transformations already afoot. Although we may be witnessing the end of a certain cycle of accumulation, along with the end of its ideological self-image and its political pecking order, the present system remains both propped up and weighed down by the cumulative weight of its obligations. That is why debt as such appears to be both the cause and the cure of the present distress. "The core of the problem, the unavoidable truth, is that our economic system is laden with debt," write contrarian economists Nassim Nicholas Taleb and Mark Spitznagel in the *Financial Times*, trying their best to sound like prophets newly arrived from the desert.[26] Another op-ed, this one

---

24   *Ibid*, p. 202.

25   David Harvey, "Is This *Really* the End of Neoliberalism?" *Counterpunch*, March 13/15, 2009, available at: counterpunch.org/harvey03132009.html.

26   Nassim Nicholas Taleb and Mark Spitznagel, "Time to tackle the real evil: too much debt," *Financial Times*, July 14, 2009, p. 9.

by a contrarian hedge fund trader, declares that debt is "capitalism's dirty little secret."[27] That much is old news. But now that Brenner's bubbles have lost their effervescence, Arrighi's terminal crisis is behind us, and Harvey's financial junta has settled into power, we have to wonder what comes next. For our purposes it is not a matter of choosing which story is most likely to predict the future, but rather of asking how far the alignment of forces that led up to the breakdown will also preside over its aftermath.

All roads to the future lead through an immense pile of debt. Whereas earlier crises were associated with ballooning debt that was concentrated in one sector (such as the massive leveraging of corporations before the Depression or the gargantuan sovereign debts of Third World countries), the latest crisis was built upon debts of all kinds, contracted for various, often conflicting reasons. What has been driving this explosion? In the first place, as we have seen, increased debt has allowed many globally competing manufacturing firms to muddle through the eighties and nineties, boosting profitability in fits and starts until it took a full-blown credit expansion to sustain them.[28] At the same time, a nearly universal but uneven increase in household debt (especially in the form of refinanced mortgages and proliferating credit cards) has boosted consumer demand in the West without sparking the long-term growth and employment that could sustain it. Public debt (as a ratio of GDP) in the G20 countries has already doubled since 1980 and looks set to rise dramatically in the coming years.[29] Finally, the financial sector pursued its speculative strategies through highly leveraged

---

27   Ben Funnell, "Debt is capitalism's dirty little secret," *Financial Times*, July 1, 2009, p. 9.
28   See David McNally, "From Financial Crisis to World-Slump: Accumulation, Financialization, and the Global Slowdown," *Historical Materialism*, Vol. 17, No. 2 (2009), pp. 35–83.
29   International Monetary Fund, "The State of Public Finances: Outlook and Medium-Term Policies After the 2008 Crisis," (Washington, D.C.: International Monetary Fund, 2009), p. 24.

borrowing, backed by what Alan Greenspan politely called "the underpricing of risk worldwide." In fact, much of that speculation was backed by precisely nothing, since the risks of failure were never calculated. Nobody on Wall Street had read Mallarmé: "A throw of the dice will never abolish chance . . ."

Yet it is important to remember that debts and obligations shape economic prospects and life possibilities in even more fundamental ways. In the most elementary sense, debts enable economic activity by liberating present resources from the most immediate pressures of productivity or profitability. Brenner's account makes clear that this enabling capacity of debts, tapped ever more desperately throughout the long downturn, has been squandered: the mass of unproductive debts on the supply side has been greatly augmented by a new mass of unproductive debts on the demand side. Insofar as all those debts will be held and enforced by a class of creditors keen to preserve the prerogatives of free-ranging capital, the only economic trend that seems certain to continue is the ongoing transfer of wealth to those who already have a lot of it. Meanwhile the basic political function of public debt—channeling resources toward socially necessary investments—has been redefined as a subsidy program to increase the power of the private sector. (How else can we explain the contortions made to avoid any talk of "nationalizing" troubled industries or public services?) With Arrighi's narrative in mind, we can see how this "structural adjustment" of public finances has played out rather badly in most places where the Washington Consensus was implemented, not least in Washington itself. Asian countries and especially China, on the other hand, have deployed the political function of debts differently, both by preserving the place of state power in the economy and by taking advantage of market opportunities to fuel development. Nevertheless, both paths lead toward an ever greater alienation of popular support as the shared debt burden grows and social provision suffers. Finally, then, we can see how debt also functions in an existential and biopolitical register. By penetrating more and more into the lifeworld and reshaping scarcity itself in its own image, indebtedness encompasses something more than the list of debts anyone happens to owe at a given moment. At the same time, it projects the twists and turns of inner life on a global scale, as if the economic system could broker a compromise between good conscience and base instincts. By forging countless short circuits between the macro and the micro, indebtedness becomes something like a whole "structure of feeling," whereby humans find themselves owing their existence (along with the lives of other beings) ever more fully to the economic apparatus that claims to control life as such.[30]

The fraught status of collectivity under capitalism can be glimpsed in an acute observation offered by Marx in *Capital*: "The only part of the so-called national wealth that actually enters into the collective possession of a modern nation is—their national debt."[31] Most people will laugh ruefully when they get the joke: the only thing that a capitalist nation can ever collectively possess, or share, is its public indebtedness. Marx clearly wants us to see how this kind of collective bond has been shaped into a tool of oppression and expropriation. Yet we will miss the dialectical force of the insight if we do not see that collective indebtedness can function as a mechanism of oppression only because it marshals a variety of cooperative relationships into a productive, constitutive force. Capital never relies on its own power alone: it secures its rule only when it can draw upon the resources of social solidarity, which it has never yet been able to exhaust. What gets called the "national debt" is really an apparatus to capture the collectivized potential wealth of a necessarily open-ended political community. The symbolic appropriation of this

---

30   For the concept of "structure of feeling," see Raymond Williams, *Marxism and Literature* (Oxford: Oxford University Press, 1997), pp. 128–35. For the concept of "apparatus" and its proximity to the concept of oikonomia, see Giorgio Agamben, "What Is an Apparatus?" in *What Is an Apparatus? and Other Essays*, trans. David Kishik and Stefan Pedatella (Palo Alto: Stanford University Press, 2009), pp. 1–24.
31   Karl Marx, *Capital*, Vol. 1, trans. Ben Fowkes (New York: Vintage Books, 1977), p. 919.

potential takes the form of "credit" issued from above, like capital "fallen from heaven," as Marx puts it. By contrast, we should reserve a special meaning of the word *indebtedness* to describe the reciprocal bonds of productivity generated between people, in their work and their lives alike—before, beyond, and through capitalist relations of production.

By definition, then, this kind of indebtedness precedes and exceeds all forms of credit. For its part, credit acquires value not through some kind of vague reciprocal "faith" between two parties but precisely because it enacts an ongoing recoding of productive powers in order to adapt them to the mechanisms of accumulation. A collective must always be "indebted" to itself in order to carry out any kind of production; it must, in other words, find durable ways to anticipate and mobilize its potential in order to realize it. As soon as the circuits of credit are coextensive with worldwide production, we can speak of a global regime of indebtedness. What characterizes capitalist societies, then, is the way that this collective indebtedness gets expressed in the generalized form of credit, which shapes and mediates relations between individuals, states, and markets, thereby subdividing and separating the collectivity that indebtedness necessarily implies. What indebtedness makes possible, credit makes profitable. Although capital always tries to take credit for everything people can do in common, its power depends at every moment upon the variable relations of force that operate between the structures of accumulation and the potentialities of indebtedness. That is why capital is always worth only as much as it can get away with, which is not everything and not forever.

By emphasizing the problem of debt in the present crisis, then, we can cut across many of the other explanations currently on offer, whether those highlight the hubris of financiers, the folly of borrowers, the irrationality of the institutional structures, or the imbalances rooted in the international system. It might be best to say that all of those explanations are somehow true, and more: we are living through a generalized crisis of the regime of indebtedness, that ensemble of structured, codified, and lived social relations upon which the reproduction of the system depends. That is to say, this regime comprises not only the financial and legal infrastructure that upholds capitalist enterprises and imposes market constraints, but also the interwoven expectations and responsibilities that put the whole apparatus in motion. The current regime of indebtedness operates on a rather different scale, and along a greater number of axes, than earlier ones. Today it is not just the "national debt" and the provision of industrial or commercial credit that is under pressure, but also new flows of international credit, as well as various deeply penetrated kinds of household debt. At the limit we may say that the collective that is now indebted to itself has become unbounded— perhaps it is itself what some theorists have started to call the global multitude. So we are witnessing today a crisis in the way structures of credit seize, partition, and exploit the productivity of the multitude, which finally owes its powers to nothing other than itself.

All of this suggests that the very notion of "crisis" needs to be recast. We usually think that a crisis means that something has broken down or stopped working properly. The word carries alarmist, if not catastrophist, overtones. But now, in spite of the apocalyptic tone recently adopted by economists, the current crisis seems eerily quiet, resembling an economic lockdown and permanent state of exception. It is as if the system itself wants to be seen as "too big to fail," it being understood that bigness is the best defense against government regulation and popular unrest alike. Instead of imagining global capital as an orbiting unearthly power, we should see it as not only grounded in reality but also newly entrenched there, built into the ruins it leaves behind.

At the same time, the crisis has provided a few glimpses of what might happen if the economic scaffolding came apart. In such moments of danger, we need not be preoccupied with visions of imminent collapse. Instead, such moments prompt us to look at the situation with new eyes, seeing how things really work, how a generation's worth of certainties must be rethought, and how a common life can be arranged differently, based on the recognition that wealth begins and ends in what we owe to each other, anybody to everybody and everybody to anybody.

2   Inequality, Poverty, Indebtedness

Now, in the old days, it was not just the common people who were poor, but the rulers too.

—Herodotus, *The Histories*

People have been saying "The rich get richer and the poor get poorer" for a long time, but it's not clear whether the phrase still carries much of a sting. Quite the contrary: although it once sounded like a bitter complaint about the ruling order, now it often serves as a cheerful defense of it, another way of saying that everything is working just the way it is supposed to. If we do not yet hear it proclaimed by prime ministers and central bankers as a basic policy goal, that can only be because there might be some lingering embarrassment about its consequences, especially in these difficult times. Nobody disputes the first part: the rich do indeed get richer, as we will see in some detail. There is some dispute, however, over whether the poor are getter poorer, and if so, how and why. Of course, for the wealthiest people on the planet that's not an issue. They seem to believe that the rich live a blessed life and that if the poor get poorer, that's only natural. Others offer a more modest version of that idea. They acknowledge that the rich do tend to get richer, but they insist that the poor do not *necessarily* get poorer, so that one may express a cautious hope that some of the poor might sometimes become somewhat less poor than they used to be. Indeed, the only remaining moral justification of the current system hangs by that thread: as long as it can be argued that the poor do not always and everywhere get poorer, the rich should go ahead and keep getting as abundantly rich as they can, in good times and bad.

This small scruple—this impulse to justify the accumulation and concentration of wealth in the name of ameliorating, if not eradicating, widespread poverty—offers a crucial hint about the current legitimations of global capitalism and, indeed, about the weakening need to legitimate it at all. The prevailing discourse may be apologetic about the specifics but remains unapologetic about the overriding vision: even if the free markets do not function perfectly, everyone is supposed to agree that capitalist models of growth remain the only hope for rich and poor alike. The pursuit of wealth can represent the very essence and purpose of human civilization only because poverty has been recast as something left over from someone else's history. In the face of metastasizing glass-box skylines and the endlessly televised worship of luxury, poverty appears to be the flawed and fallen condition of life without capitalism. The fact of poverty will be acknowledged only in order to make those wretched people somehow more pathetic or pathological, whether glimpsed from a distance or demonized as an immediate threat. Even when poverty is recognized as a persistent human problem, it will be explained in localized terms and addressed on a case-by-case basis, as if countries were poor because of their own particular disadvantages, and individuals because of bad habits they haven't learned to break. State-of-the-art capitalism—the multilayered tangle of markets enforced by its biggest powers—can solve the problem (the story goes) only if everyone will see it as the cure rather than the cause of poverty. That is why the most optimistic plans for helping the poor scarcely mention the existence of massively concentrated wealth, let alone suggest that such wealth is part of the sickness, too.

Yet it should be clear that there is no way to "fix" poverty without "fixing" the processes of accumulation. Without dismantling the top-heavy structures of the world's economic architecture, poverty reduction programs and deficit-driven fiscal policies can do little to reverse the entrenched patterns of inequality. Moreover, entrepreneurial schemes to help the poor all too often follow the priorities set by the developed countries, thereby preserving the prerogatives of capital and launching another round of lopsided accumulation. As the current crisis has demonstrated once more, and with renewed ferocity, the global system has imposed deeper forms of dependency without cultivating stronger forms of reciprocity: the virtuous circle of commerce always turns vicious when left to its own devices, and unequal booms unerringly lead to even more unequal busts.

Instead of treating inequality as inevitable and poverty as some kind of immature condition, we should start by seeing both as the result of an ongoing process—actual impoverishment—that is systemically produced and maintained by the current arrangement of things. The basic mechanisms of impoverishment—expropriation and oppression, rooted in violence—have been at work for centuries, administered by a variety of social forms and political regimes in increasingly multilateral and overdetermined ways. In the course of this long history there has been a fundamental shift in the meaning of poverty: whereas it might once have been rooted in sheer scarcity external to social organization (and therefore would have seemed natural, local, and ineradicable) it is now permanently installed in the global functioning of the system, as the price a certain portion of the population must pay for the enrichment of the rest. Whether this shift from contingent scarcity to structural deprivation and exclusion occurred during the Mesolithic era or during postmodernity does not matter very much (that depends upon one's conception of capitalism as a world system); what we face today is a thoroughly contemporary system for the production and maintenance of widespread poverty for the sake of stupendous wealth.

Debates over poverty and inequality hinge upon economic factors that can be measured as well as existential valences that cannot. The difficulty cannot be resolved by multiplying indicators of well-being and deprivation, as economists usually do: mere survival cannot be averaged with opulence, and the threat of genocide cannot be tallied in life expectancy figures. Once a price has been put on what is lacking, the struggles of history disappear and even the worst situations appear subject to utilitarian calculation. Nor can this difficulty be resolved in the other direction, as philosophers have tried, by treating poverty qualitatively, as a state of bare existence, something like the material and spiritual zero degree of humanity, always on the brink of annihilation or renewal. The economist who quantifies it risks rendering poverty fungible; the philosopher who makes it a quality of existence risks sanctifying or eternalizing it. Yet both approaches offer a moment of truth: the problems of poverty and inequality signal the irreducibly biopolitical dimension of the struggles around the current regime of capital. That is why wealth and poverty cannot be distinguished on strictly quantitative grounds, nor can they be opposed as qualitative opposites: these terms pose for us a problem of knowledge that we should not be too quick to resolve. In the process of asking how we know what we think we know about the world, we will have to put to use, even while calling into question, empirical measurements and philosophical concepts alike.

Numbers

The main argument here is simple: we begin by examining the facts on the ground established by the current system of accumulation, emphasizing inequality's enduring monumental topographies rather than its transient, marginal trends. We need to survey the current structure of wealth in its gross dimensions, even if the specific policies and practices that have built this structure may be now in the process of being reformed or at least repackaged. (As we saw in the previous chapter, the slogans of neoliberalism may soon fade away, but the stockpiles of loot it created will not disappear so easily.) By placing ourselves self-consciously at a turning point—in the midst of a great crisis—we can get a clearer perspective on the questions that will dominate the years ahead. Can the current system rescue itself and carry on as before? Will the prevailing patterns of inequality persist, or worsen, even as blocs of wealth are destroyed? Could there be a destruction of wealth large enough—coupled with a realignment of political forces bold enough—to open up a different kind of future?

Although everybody on earth is surrounded by the evidence every day, it is hard to get a grasp of the drastically warped contours of contemporary capitalism. Statistics concerning the distribution of income, wealth, and poverty are always key exhibits in debates over globalization, where they form the backbone for a series of rather schematic oppositions. For some commentators, these figures are the clearest evidence of the injustice of the current system; for others, they offer proof that the world has been enjoying a golden age of rising prosperity. The differences between these two positions have only sharpened since the onset of the global crisis. Yet insofar as both positions call upon the same data (or rather, variations of the same kinds of data), we need to ask how the apparent objectivity of the numbers can obscure both shared premises and fundamental disagreements. The construction of data is never strictly technical, and debates over numbers always open onto essentially political differences over basic principles and goals.

In the first place, statistics about the uneven accumulation of wealth necessarily invoke a principle of *equality*, whether couched in theories of distributional justice or simple notions of fairness and decency. Quite apart from whatever it might mean as a political ideal or goal, equality seems like a neutral standard: given a certain population and a certain quantity of values, it should be an easy matter to calculate how much equality there is. To speak of equality on a global scale likewise seems straightforward: the measurement of inequality records the relative resources and accomplishments of various populations. Such measurements, however, acquire a new and salient significance as soon as one assumes that the world has been effectively integrated as a single unified economy. Only with the advent of neoliberal globalization has the economic and social texture of the world been sufficiently homogenized that the measurement of inequality might really serve as a useful descriptor of systemic processes. Yet equality has been repudiated as a political goal almost everywhere, so it should be no surprise that the evidence for any systemic leveling is especially weak. In particular, the idea that there is any strong correlation between neoliberal policies and equality is getting harder and harder to sustain, even for the IMF.[1] For the staunchest champions of the current system, inequality figures are simply irrelevant: an equitable distribution of prosperity was never part of the agenda. On the other hand, there are many critics who see the persistence and growth of gross inequality as the best proof of the immorality and unworkability of the current system. Peter Singer, for example, has persuasively argued that the project of globalization has failed to live up to its grounding metaphor: it has not created "one world" in any generative sense, because the material gains of economic integration and mutual dependence have not been shared in egalitarian ways.[2]

Along a different axis and in a less obvious way, statistics measuring poverty are often treated as an inverted index of *freedom*, on the assumption that the poor are trapped by necessity and the wealthy are

---

[1]   See International Monetary Fund, *Global Economic Outlook: Globalization and Inequality* (October 2007), especially Chapter 4. In explaining the rise of inequality, the report puts most of the blame on "technological progress," saying that "[globalization] has had a much smaller disequalizing impact overall" (p. 159). Giovanni Arrighi puts the matter more clearly when he points out that one must set the positive accomplishments of China and India against "the long series of economic disasters that actual adherence to these [Washington Consensus] prescriptions have provoked in sub-Saharan Africa, Latin America, and the former USSR." *Adam Smith in Beijing* (London: Verso, 2008), p. 354.

[2]   See Peter Singer, *One World: The Ethics of Globalization* (New Haven: Yale University Press, 2004).

liberated by affluence. Proponents of neoliberal globalization tend to draw this correlation very tightly, seeing a reduction in poverty figures as a sign that a country is encouraging an atmosphere of economic freedom and openness. In particular, the people of China and India are said to have enjoyed a new and irresistible wave of freedom as their GDP has climbed in recent decades. Those who praise such achievements on behalf of globalization do not like to notice that inequality has been widening in those countries as well. Likewise, they rarely differentiate between, let alone endorse, the political systems that brought about these changes. In fact, few mainstream commentators have a kind word to say about state power anywhere, and it seems long ago that anybody trusted the state to serve as a bulwark against the global system. Those who insist on the strictly political causes of poverty—tabulating "corruption indices" and "democracy ratings" to prove that bad governance is most to blame—tend to be the same people who think that governments should exist mainly to enforce the prescriptions of the market, and thus that the best measure of a government's performance is its ability to raise capital from the international bond markets. Critics (such as Amartya Sen) object that the promise of formal or atmospheric freedoms is insufficient without genuine democratic empowerment. Sen proposes to define poverty as the deprivation of the basic human capabilities that alone can sustain the "substantive" freedom to lead one's life. Thus "development" must offer more than improved economic conditions; it must become the enabling process of social growth itself, "a momentous engagement with freedom's possibilities."[3]

---

3   Amartya Sen, *Development as Freedom* (New York: Anchor Books, 1999), p. 298. See also Sen's two-page comment on "the role of values in capitalism," concluding with this verdict: "But within its domain, capitalism works effectively through a system of ethics that provides the vision and the trust needed for successful use of the market mechanism and related institutions" (p. 263). The theme of "trust" as the glue of social relations corresponds to a benign notion of the market as something stemming from individual values. As this essay argues, "indebtedness" and "solidarity" would be better names for what binds societies together, requiring a thorough rethinking of what "market mechanisms" can and cannot do.

If the critique of the global economy in terms of equality shows us just how far short we have fallen, the critique in terms of freedom shows just how far we have to go. In fact, these two terms provide fundamentally different perspectives on the situation. Equality can serve as a strict and practical principle, a goal that allows for a variety of strategies. Freedom, however much it might have advanced in specific ways, stands as an eternally transcendent ideal. (That is why grafting the idea of wealth onto that of freedom seems like such a dishonest ideological maneuver: freedom loses its universal critical edge and becomes an excuse to inflict servitude on others.) Following a suggestion from Alain Badiou, we should open a place here for the third term in the classic slogan of the French Revolution: along with *égalité* and *liberté* there must be *fraternité*, or solidarity. As Badiou explains, using Lacanian terms: if equality takes the Imaginary position, "since it cannot come about as an objective figure," and liberty takes the Symbolic position, "since it is the presupposed instrument, the fecund negative," what we will call solidarity takes the position of the Real, "that which is sometimes encountered, in the here and now."[4] It is not at all obvious how solidarity might be reckoned in the ledger books of world history: we will have to return to this question after we have a better account of the current global situation.

The ongoing debates over the balance sheets of contemporary globalization revolve around various kinds of evidence, and we can only trace the outlines here. Quite apart from the different ideological interests at work, there are treacherous methodological difficulties at every level. For our purposes, we will aim for a general snapshot of the current situation, in order to survey what kind of world has been brought together by the latest round of globalization. In this way we can get a clearer idea not only of the state of official research, but also of the polemical contexts in which that research plays its part. The material is organized around apparently simple

---

4   Alain Badiou, *The Century*, trans. Alberto Toscano (Cambridge: Polity Press, 2007), p. 102.

questions: How "big" are poverty and inequality, both within various countries and across the global system? Have poverty and inequality been growing or shrinking in recent years? By drawing up an economic report card, we can draw up a balance sheet for the dominant years of the neoliberal project, up until the moment when its forward momentum was decisively halted.

Before going any further, it is important to consider how the numbers are measured and expressed. There are various techniques for generating statistics about income and wealth, as well as different benchmarks for counting the poor. Much of this research is produced by economists in and around the World Bank and the United Nations.[5] Income per capita, the most frequently cited statistic in inequality reports, can be calculated using either national account figures, household survey data, or some stylized combination of the two. Each set of data carries its own assumptions about what "income" is and what its measured level can tell us about the welfare of people. Should "income" be calculated as a share of national income, or as household disposable income? Or would it be more relevant to measure household consumption and expenditure? Working from one angle, one could try to count all of the work that people do, whether paid in wages or not; from the other, one could try to account for everything people acquire and use to carry out their lives. Having chosen an angle, one must then consider the time frame. Whereas income and consumption distribution figures are necessarily expressed as an annual amount, wealth distribution figures try to capture the results of ongoing accumulation, which, while generally harder to pin down, are obviously crucial when considering the social rigidities of the system. There are many

---

5 See Eoin Callan, "World Bank 'uses doubtful evidence to push policies,'" *Financial Times*, December 22, 2006, p. 4. The "first big external audit of the bank's use of research," led by Kenneth Rogoff and Angus Deaton, found that the bank had dismissed unfavorable research, especially with respect to the costs of trade liberalization.

reports about the wealth of the very rich (from *Forbes* magazine, Merrill Lynch, etc.), but it is much harder to track the distribution of wealth across the board; that requires a large and consistent set of survey data. (We will look at one example shortly.) As if these difficulties were not enough, it is worth noting that the household surveys currently available do not provide any information about the inequality *within* households, a gender and age gap that goes some way toward falsifying these statistical images of global poverty at the outset. In sum, every pool of evidence—national accounts, tax returns, censuses, and surveys—involves different limitations and distortions, especially at the opposite ends of the economic hierarchy.

Likewise, basic decisions made when rendering the numbers can tilt them in significant ways. It is common to use "purchasing price parity" [PPP] exchange rates to compare figures from country to country (as opposed to official or market exchange rates between currencies), but there are several markedly different ways to generate PPP rates. This issue deserves more than technical scrutiny. A PPP rate is generated by comparing the price of a "consumption basket" of goods and services in different countries. The method depends on the composition of a "basket" that would generalize the consumption habits of people in different countries, as well as those of rich and poor people within each country: obviously, the very act of composing the common measure begins to erase the vital differences that are being compared. What things does everybody buy? What services does everybody use? Should international comparisons be drawn from the bottom up, using a PPP basket weighted toward food items likely to be bought by the poor, or from the top down, with a basket weighted toward higher-cost services that the rich are more likely to purchase? Measuring income and wealth in PPP rates, as opposed to current exchange rates, will register much higher levels of output in poorer countries, but at the same time will be misleading if we want to know how different currencies exert different degrees of command on the world scale. A dollar is not a dollar when it is really a peso or a yuan; likewise a yuan is not just a yuan when it can buy dollars, and thereby drive their value up or down. "Purchasing power," like "investing power," depends greatly on which currency you actually hold: some currencies have a strictly local range while others exercise a truly global reach. Thus we see how numbers can encode divergent political perspectives: there is a basic difference between measuring value in terms of everyday life and measuring its power in terms of global capital. Finally, it is crucial to keep in mind that none of these tools can properly measure the goods and activities that do not pass through the market mechanism (including public provisions and collective resources). As we will see later, this factor is especially important.

Of all the shorthand abstractions used by economists to register inequality, the most common is the Gini index (also called the Gini coefficient), which expresses in a single number the degree of inequality across a particular set of people, whether one is examining a kindergarten class or the state of Kenya. That is to say, the Gini refers only to the distribution curve of income or wealth, and does not indicate how wealthy or how poor people actually are. It expresses an abstract relationship, not the degree of welfare.[6] For example, Australia and Sri Lanka have approximately equal Gini distributions, but with very different average levels of income. A Gini score of 1 would signify perfect equality (everybody has the same share), while a score of 100 would signify perfect inequality (one person has everything and everybody else has nothing). The higher the number, the more top-heavy the spread. Apart from various technical shortcomings that need not detain us here, it is a hard number to grasp

---

6   The Gini coefficient measures the deviation from a perfectly equal "distribution frequency," represented as a line rising at a straight 45-degree angle (Gini=0). A data set plotting the distribution of values (say, incomes) across a population (say, households) will render a more or less regular "Lorenz curve" beneath the line of equality: thus the Gini measures the deviation without describing its shape. It is worth noting that this measurement assumes that there are no negative values, i.e., that no household would have negative income.

intuitively or to interpret politically. If a Gini score of 1 corresponds to a commonsense notion of fairness, and a score of 100 signals the ultimate despotism, the scores in between will always seem more or less unfair, more or less intolerable and indefensible. In that respect, Gini numbers can serve as a useful ideological Rorschach test: just how much inequality can we excuse or explain away?

With all of those caveats in mind, we can now ask: how unequal is the world? How poor are people? The first answers probably have to be: More unequal than you can see, and Poorer than you think.

Wealth and (in)equality

In 2006 Branko Milanovic, an economist then working for the World Bank, wrote a paper in which he calculated that global income inequality measures around 65 Gini points.[7] That figure is larger than the inequality found in any individual country: that is to say, income distribution throughout the world economy as a whole is rather more unequal than in any national economy. By comparison, the domestic income inequality of the US is 41 and the UK is 36; India comes in at 37, Russia at 40, and China at 47. The low end of the scale includes Japan and several Scandinavian countries at 25, and the high end includes Brazil, South Africa, Botswana, and Bolivia, scoring from 57 to 60. Speaking broadly, Gini scores in higher-income countries are around half or less of the global score, ranging across the upper 20s, 30s, or low 40s. Middle-income countries tend to be somewhat more unequal than that, and the most unequal countries can be found in Latin America and Africa.[8]

---

7   Branko Milanovic, "Global Income Inequality: What it is and why it matters," World Bank Policy Research Working Paper, March 2006, p. 14.

8   The Gini scores (rounded to whole numbers) have been taken from United Nations Development Program, *Human Development Report, 2007/2008* (New York: Palgrave Macmillan, 2007). Henceforth cited as HDR07.

What does a global Gini of 65 actually mean? In his paper, Milanovic explains it this way:

> [The] top 5 percent of individuals in the world receive about 1/3 of total world income, and the top 10 percent one half. If we take the bottom 5 and 10 percent, they receive respectively 0.2 and 0.7 percent of world total income. That means that the ratio between the average income received by the richest 5 percent and the poorest 5 percent is 165 to 1. The richest people earn in about 48 hours what the poorest earn in a year.[9]

Notice how Milanovic translates the Gini number in three different ways, expressing inequality using percentages, proportions, and earning power. Such formulations are a familiar feature in discussions about the distribution of income, where there seems to be no single perspective from which these abstract indices can make sense. Mathematics must give way to metaphor. Everybody knows that there are "rich" and "poor" people in every country, and that the "rich" in one place would be "poor" somewhere else, but it is difficult to gauge that imbalance precisely because the geographical and statistical distances between pockets of the rich and everybody else have been widening. The world economy has developed in such a way that the local or national frameworks in which inequality is usually perceived, experienced, and fought over have generally become not only more unequal in themselves, but more incommensurable with one another. So although these statistics present global inequality in individual terms, the phenomenon itself cannot

---

9   Milanovic, "Global Income Inequality," p. 16. Here Milanovic uses PPP values. It might be worth noting that in the Roman Empire, circa 14 AD, the top 1.5 percent of the population (the emperor, senators, knights, decurions, and others, totaling about 330,000 people) took 26 percent of the total income of the Empire. That proportion is not much more unequal than the figures cited by Milanovic. See Angus Maddison, *Contours of the World Economy, 1–2030 AD: Essays in Macro-Economic History* (Oxford: Oxford University Press, 2007), p. 50.

be grasped at the scale of individual rewards or punishments. What might appear to each of us as vicissitudes of fate and fortune are actually organized by more durable relationships and processes that usually remain opaque. As a matter of convention, statistics take the perspective of average individuals, households, nations, or groups of nations, but none of these angles can capture the way structural forms of inequality cut across every social aggregate from the largest to the smallest, worlds within worlds of disparity and deprivation.

The picture looks even more imbalanced when we measure wealth instead of income. In 2006, a detailed study of global wealth distribution from the UN University's World Institute for Development Economics Research (WIDER) calculated the worldwide wealth Gini score, measured in purchasing power, at 80 points.[10] That is higher than all but a few of individual countries' scores. (The high end of the scale, 80 and above, is shared by the US, Switzerland, and a few places like Namibia and Zimbabwe, although data is lacking for a few places like Qatar.) Both at a global level and within individual countries, the UNU researchers found that "wealth distribution is more unequal than income."[11] That conclusion might seem obvious, but it remains difficult to get a sense of the discrepancies at stake. For example, while the US income distribution Gini is 41, its wealth distribution Gini is 80: drastically more unequal. Worldwide, the top 10 percent of adults take half of all income, but they own almost three-quarters of the assets; the top 5 percent take a third of the income, but hold more than half of the wealth. And if we express these values at official exchange rates (in order to register their current market force), the disparities appear even more drastic: in that case the global Gini is 89, higher than for even the most corrupt

---

10   James B. Davies, Susanna Sandstrom, Anthony Shorrocks, Edward N. Wolff, "The World Distribution of Household Wealth," United Nations University, World Institute for Development Economics Research, 2008, p. 16. Available online: wider.unu.edu.

11   *Ibid*, p. 9.

countries. That is the score that would be assigned to "a 100-person population in which one person receives $900 and the remaining 99 people each receive $1."[12] The report confirms that there is an especially steep concentration at the very top, where "members of the top decile are almost 400 times richer, on average, than the bottom 50 percent, and members of the top percentile are almost 2,000 times richer." There is no gently sloping middle ground, either. The middle 60 percent (leaving aside the top and bottom quintiles) owns a mere 6 percent of total assets. (This vast population is the fabled "emergent global bourgeoisie" so often invoked by free market enthusiasts.) Or to see it from another angle: the entire bottom half of the world's adults (more than 1.8 billion people) hold "barely 1 percent of global wealth."[13]

That is how things stood for the rich at the brink of the financial crisis. No doubt there has been significant destruction of paper wealth since then. But has there been a reversal of inequality? Or will the wealthiest manage to maintain their advantages? The earliest signs suggested that the erosion of wealth has been significant but is likely to be temporary. The 2009 World Wealth Report from Merrill Lynch/Capgemini found that the world's richest people ("high net worth individuals," defined as those with financial assets over $1 million, numbering about 8.6 million people) owned assets worth about $32.8 trillion dollars, down about 20 percent from 2008.[14] Yet that decline brings their collective worth only back to 2005 levels, a sign that this group had been reaping higher than average gains all along. Meanwhile the very rich—"ultra high net worth individuals," those with at least $30 million each in financial assets—lost about 24 percent from their highs, undoing the past few years of outsize

---

12   *Ibid*, p. 7.

13   *Ibid*. For the "middle" deciles, see the chart on page 14.

14   Megan Murphy, "Credit crunch cuts swathe through ranks of the super-rich," *Financial Times*, June 25, 2009, and Peter Thal Larsen, "World's rich reduce property exposure to dodge credit crisis," *Financial Times*, June 25, 2008.

gains. Yet the 2009 report offers solace to the wealthiest, predicting that their collective financial wealth will grow again, to $48.5 trillion in four years, although the overall population of such individuals will be markedly smaller than before. Even among the ranks of the wealthiest individuals, the ruthless processes of winnowing and hoarding will intensify.[15] North America will continue to amass the largest bloc of concentrated wealth, although the Asia-Pacific region is supposed to take the lead by 2012. In contrast to the sprawling imponderables of poverty, the answer to the question "Who owns the world?" is still remarkably plain. Indeed, it is getting easier to name names.

For thirty years or more, the mantra has been "a rising tide lifts all boats." As a description of what has happened through globalization, this is clearly untrue. Year by year, the mechanisms of accumulation have dumped greater shares of wealth into the laps of fewer people. As Robert Hunter Wade of the London School of Economics put it: "world inequality has risen since the early 1980s . . . [and] the absolute size of the income gap between countries is widening rapidly."[16] The economists Gérard Duménil and Dominique Lévy conclude their study of wealth polarization and growth rates in starker terms, arguing that "the strengthening of power of the upper fractions of ruling classes was detrimental to growth, everywhere, be it in their own countries or in the periphery."[17] That is especially true in the United States, where the past three decades have seen a massive shift of wealth upward while overall growth rates lagged behind the previous, somewhat more equally distributed, economic era. Now

15 For recent trends among the superrich, see Robert Frank, "Millionaire Population Drops 15%," *Wall Street Journal*, June 24, 2009. Available online: blogs .wsj.com/wealth.

16 Robert Hunter Wade, "Poverty and Income Distribution: What Is the Evidence?" in Ann Pettifor, editor, *Real World Economic Outlook* (New York and London: Palgrave Macmillan, 2003), p. 147.

17 Gérard Duménil and Dominique Lévy, "The Neoliberal (Counter)Revolution" in A. Saad Filho and D. Johnson, *Neoliberalism: A Critical Reader* (London: Pluto Press, 2005).

the real question has become: Does an ebbing tide sink all boats? Will the global downswing bring about a more equal distribution of wealth? In light of the picture drawn here, it would seem that even the most aggressive redistributionist measures—none of which are under serious consideration among the managers of the world economy—would have a hard time chipping away at the well-entrenched results of the accumulation system. For all the insight it offers into the current functioning of the system, the optics of inequality may not allow us to see what it would take to make a real change.

Sooner or later, every attempt to measure the gap between wealth and poverty will produce a kind of split vision, seeing the poor in terms of how little they can consume and the rich in terms of how much they can accumulate. As the data make plain, the economic sphere is not a sphere at all, but an unstable antagonism split between two different thresholds: on one side, fixing the price of staying alive for people who might not survive; on the other, assigning a value to the power of capital to transcend life in order to rule over it. Between these extremes there can be no equal exchange and no common ground, but only the confrontation between the command structures of credit on one side and the webs of indebtedness on the other. We will come back to this point later.

The economic parallax transects the political domain as well. In practice the principle of equality can be invoked a thousand times a day, always compromised and qualified, in the service of maintaining some version of inequality. By contrast, the goal of universal equality as such, which would abolish the autonomy of the economy, currently plays no role in politics anywhere. Displaced into the orbit of media rhetoric and moral ideals, it is nevertheless praised in some circles as a cosmopolitan ideal, honored precisely because there is no responsible authority or agency capable of realizing such a vision. Jagdish Bhagwati, an evangelist of free markets, dismisses the very idea of measuring global inequality for this reason: he argues that there is no "addressee" to whom such numbers would provide useful information. There is an unreal vantage point built into the statistics themselves, as if there were something like a global legislative body or taxation authority capable of redressing the imbalances. That is exactly what Bhagwati does not want. And, in this sense, he is right: there is indeed no responsible power governing the world economy. At the moment we lack even the political vocabulary to designate a collective addressee of an egalitarian politics, let alone a collective agent of an equalizing political economy. That is why remedies inspired by the principle of equality nowadays lead to impassioned pleas for philanthropic tithing or sermons of the teaching-someone-to-fish variety, but no further.

Poverty and (un)freedom

Counting the poor is a different sort of exercise. Here it is not a matter of comparing relative quantities, but of redefining a qualitative condition of being-in-the-world—*what does it mean to be poor?*—according to some standard of subsistence. Once a benchmark has been set, it becomes possible to count how many people live above and below it. The skeptics will always point out that this procedure is prone to arbitrary and cynical manipulation, forever incapable of accounting for the fundamentally subjective and psychic dimensions of immiseration. A truly relativist approach could, not without justice, find poverty everywhere: it is impossible to count the number of people who *feel* poor. Setting "the poverty line," then, like setting a "living wage" or securing "public welfare," has as much to do with struggles over political discourse as with demography. (The use of PPP rates for comparisons adds additional complexities: because food is one of the major components of the consumption basket, the calculation of a PPP embeds a series of assumptions about nutrition and health.) In the major media, the World Bank's definition of global poverty has become the most frequently used benchmark: those who live on less than about $1.25 a day (at PPP exchange rates) are considered poor. (Although this benchmark was recently raised, it is still often cited as "a dollar a day.") In 2008, the Bank estimated that 1.4 billion people, out of 6.7 billion total, were living below the international poverty line. The Bank also measures the number of people living below about $2 a day: another 1.1 billion fell into that category, living on something between $1.25 and $2 a day.[18]

The $1.25- and $2-a-day benchmarks differentiate "extreme" and "moderate" poverty, respectively, in an effort to distinguish between more and less severe degrees of destitution.[19] In fact, one does not hear very much about "moderate" poverty: for the purposes of most media coverage, poverty isn't poverty unless it is extreme. At either level, the Bank's poverty lines are meant to be seen as a convenient abstraction rather than an attempt to dictate what poor people actually need.[20] The national poverty lines set by developing countries' governments can vary significantly from the international poverty threshold. For example, Honduras reports that 51 percent of its population lives below its poverty line, while the Bank calculates that 22 percent of Hondurans consume less than $1 a day. It can work the other way, too: the Bank's measurements put 75 percent of Mozambique's population in "extreme poverty," while Mozambique's own definition of "poverty" puts the figure at 54 percent: two rather divergent views of the same set of people at roughly the same time. In the majority of cases, the national poverty line falls somewhere between $1 and $2 a day, placing more people below the locally determined poverty line than the Bank's headline poverty count.[21] Given the conflicting interests at stake in producing these figures, it

18   World Bank, *World Economic Indicators: Poverty Data* (Washington, D.C.: World Bank, 2008), p. 10.

19   Jeffrey Sachs, *The End of Poverty: Economic Possibilities for Our Time* (New York: Penguin Press, 2005), p. 20.

20   World Bank, *World Development Report 2000/2001: Attacking Poverty,* (Washington, D.C.: World Bank, 2000), pp. 17 and 320. In using these numbers, it is important to bear in mind the cautions raised by Robert Wade in the essay cited in note 16, above.

21   HDR07, Table 3, pp. 238–40.

is easy to see why the poverty count would be distorted, most often by undercounting, but it is hard to know what the more accurate total might be. Pundits and editorialists have recently adopted the easy cliché that there are a billion poor people, casually rounding off 400 million from the World Bank's already minimal number. Perhaps "one billion" or "one sixth of humanity" corresponds to an ideological comfort zone: from the perspective of the current world-picture it is big enough to seem like a problem but not big enough to sound too dangerous or unmanageable. It delimits "their" deprivation without acknowledging its proximity to "our" way of life—an accursed share the rest of us can live with. But as long as we insist upon drawing a poverty line, it would be more honest to reverse the proportions: the "bottom" 6 billion people have much more in common with each other than they do with the "top" 700 million, who, as we've seen, command more than half the world's total income and about three-quarters of its total wealth. Set against the total wealth of the earth and all of its people, poverty should be seen as the norm, not the exception.

While the World Bank defines poverty in largely economic terms, the annual UN Human Development Report tries to measure what it calls "human poverty." Its data track dozens of indicators, including such diverse markers as immunization rates, nourishment levels, education expenditure, condom use, Internet access, unemployment, and prison populations, as well as a variety of gender inequities. Out of those, the report selects and synthesizes three key indicators—life expectancy, literacy and education levels, and per capita GDP—to create a "human development index" [HDI] for each country. The HDI is meant to provide a "powerful alternative to GDP per capita as a summary measure of human well-being," giving equal weight to health, wealth, and knowledge.[22] The results are tabulated and ranked—in 2007 Iceland was at the top, Sierra Leone at

---

22   HDR07, p. 225.

the bottom—and then arranged into three groups representing high, medium, and low human development. By this reckoning, about 1.6 billion people live in high, 4.2 billion in medium, and 650 million in low human development countries.[23] The report also calculates a "human poverty index" measuring curtailed life expectancy, underweight children, usage of unimproved water, and adult illiteracy rates; for developed countries, the long-term unemployment rate is added to the index as an indicator of "social exclusion."[24] Because the data are processed into national averages, these indices give a fairly vague sense of inequality, blurring differences between individuals or groups. Poverty is thus defined as a relative deficit of development, expressed through an array of measures, rendered as composite scores, and seen through the lens of each country's comparative achievement. At this level of abstraction, it appears that average levels of health, wealth, and education are advancing across the board: over the past fifteen years, the HDI figures for most countries have been steadily rising. Some countries, however, are suffering from outright regression, falling back from previous levels. (They are clustered in central and southern Africa and the former USSR, with populations totaling at least 440 million people.) The recent trends of progress, as broad as they are, have been unsteady and unevenly distributed.

If we focus on "headline" or "extreme" poverty, the picture looks rather less good. The Human Development Report devotes special attention to monitoring the UN's Millennium Development Goals (MDGs), the eight-point program of global improvements adopted in 2000 "to create an environment—at the national and global levels alike—which is conducive to development and the elimination of

---

23   Note that the rankings and groupings set apart the worst cases (22 nations) from the large middle and the high groupings (85 and 70 countries, respectively). The scores on which these divisions are based seem especially arbitrary: above 0.8; between 0.79 and 0.51; below 0.5. If the bottom threshold were raised to 0.6, the lower group would more than double, to 46, with an additional 631 million people.

24   HDR07, p. 357.

poverty."[25] The first goal on the list is "eradicate extreme poverty and hunger," with the short-term target of cutting in half, by 2015, the proportion of people in extreme poverty. There are seven other Millennium Development Goals, addressing education, gender equality, child mortality, maternal health, diseases including HIV, environmental sustainability, and—the most extensive of all— economic development. In most instances, the goals include specific targets measured in the Human Development Report. (For example: "Goal 2: Achieve universal primary education. Ensure that, by 2015, children everywhere, boys and girls alike, will be able to complete a full course of primary schooling.") There are no further prescriptions attached: the 189 member-nations of the UN have agreed to meet these goals, using whatever means available. The eighth goal, however, "Develop a global partnership for development," with seven specific targets, is more sweeping, more policy-driven, lacking any deadlines, and therefore open to interminable negotiations. Its package of financial infrastructure reforms, debt relief, employment quotas, drug access, technological expansion, and other items was evidently designed to set the conditions within which the other goals would be met. With the onset of the global crisis, all of the predictions have come undone, and it is unclear whether *any* of the major goals will be fully met.[26] The main elements of the economic agenda in particular have been decisively derailed. In the years since 2000, the members of the UN—whether functioning all together as the UN or in smaller groupings such as the Organization for Economic Cooperation and Development (OECD), the WTO, the IMF, the World Bank, the Asian Development Bank, the European Union, the African Union, etc.—have been far from united in their commitment to pursue a common strategy to address poverty, provide devel-

---

25   HDR07, pp. 383–4.

26   United Nations, *The Millennium Development Goals Report* (New York: United Nations, 2009). The report takes pains to show how the global economic crisis may undo the progress already made and set new obstacles to further improvements.

opment aid, or alter the rules of the trading system. As the downturn deepens, any kind of concerted action on such issues looks increasingly unlikely, despite ever more urgent appeals.

Here we return to the idea that the fight against poverty necessarily invokes the principle of freedom. At best, this linkage affirms the ancient principle that self-sufficiency is the basic condition of liberty. At worst, the invocation of freedom serves as an all-purpose abstraction to justify new kinds of dependency. In practice, the call of freedom gets lost in translation somewhere between the lofty heights of wealth and the vast shoals of impoverishment. Which freedoms count most, for whom? The economic clauses of the UN Millennium Declaration are couched in the language of "market access" and "opportunity," while the World Bank's 2000 report on poverty opens with an endorsement of "the fundamental freedoms of action and choice."[27] Are these the only freedoms that matter in the global system? Are these really freedoms at all?

From the vantage point of capitalism, which is the vanishing point of infinite accumulation, everybody lives in a deficit of the grand freedoms that only capital itself can enjoy—for what is the power of capital, if not "action" and "choice" elevated to inhuman eminence? But from the vantage point of the laboring multitudes, the most basic freedom is that which people make together and give to each other so that all of us can live. The law of the market, which presents itself as a transcendent "freedom of freedoms," actually travesties the notions of "law" and "freedom" alike. As the crisis of the globalized markets deepens, everybody may learn once more that freedom is only free when it can break from the regime of unfreedom erected in its name. That is the grain of truth in the conjunction of "development" and "freedom": in marshalling the resources and capabilities needed to survive the ongoing crisis, people reclaim for their own lives a sense of purpose that had previously been programmed by

---

27   World Bank, *World Development Report 2000/2001: Attacking Poverty*, p. 1.

the imperatives of capital. They decide what they want to do, they move where they want to go, they live with the greatest indifference to currency exchanges and stock markets. For the moment, that kind of freedom remains most rare of all, manifested in scattered efforts to build self-organizing networks and countereconomic enclaves. And so we find that the principles of equality and freedom, once seen as mutually reinforcing, now tend to work in opposite directions: the ethical appeal to bind ourselves as one world will have no hold on people who see no better choice than the most radical liberations, withdrawal, and exodus.

Fraternité in absentia

It would be a fine thing if we could round out this overview of the global economic situation by completing the famous slogan of the French Revolution: after *égalité* and *liberté* must come *fraternité*. But *fraternité*—in the sense of collective belongingness and solidarity—cannot be measured by official statistics. That does not mean that it has ceased to be a real force. On the contrary, we can get a sense of the current state of solidarity by measuring its absence, or more precisely, by surveying the various ways in which solidarity has been appropriated and turned against itself. The other face of *fraternité* is indebtedness, which is why we can search for a kind of reverse image of contemporary solidarity by examining the ligatures of credit and debt that incessantly attempt to bind people's lives to the tracks of capital.

In other words, we might take the aggregate level of debts as a notation, if not an expression, of a collective capacity to augment present powers out of the material, imaginary, and symbolic resources mobilized by the whole system. For the purposes of this hypothesis, it does not matter that these resources are mobilized through unequal and unfree means. In fact, the map of indebtedness provides a kind of X-ray of both the bare-bones requirements of maintaining the system and of its most extravagant excesses. It is a matter of sizing up *what humankind, bound together, is actually capable of*—in the best and worst senses of that phrase at once. Thus indebtedness marks the Real of solidarity in several distinct senses: in the way it sustains material production, in the way it signifies a domain of dependency and sharing otherwise inaccessible, and in the way it seals our belonging to the world through our being with others (we need to know that we're all "in the soup," as Sartre used to say).

As a matter of bookkeeping, debt is usually distinguished according to several broad categories, depending on who is borrowing what from whom. A government borrows by issuing *public debt*. Everything else can be called *private debt*, which is in turn divided between two sectors: *businesses* and *households*. Each of these sectors engages in many kinds of debt. Public debt includes national (federal or sovereign) debt alongside borrowing by local, regional, or state governments. Business debt includes the whole array of borrowing for commercial, investment, and speculative purposes, whether corporate or noncorporate: official statistics distinguish between *nonfinancial* and *financial* entities depending on each borrower's main kind of activity (which is often a fuzzy issue). Finally, household debt includes mortgages for houses, car loans, student loans, credit card debt, and any other kind of borrowing that people can dream up. Yet these classifications cover only the debtor's side of the arrangement. To get a more complete picture, it is necessary to account for the different types of creditor, to distinguish between domestic or foreign sources and destinations of credit, and to examine the various types and durations of debt instrument. The credit market as a whole circulates through all of these sectors, lifting each on the leverage of the others. Insofar as it works, it transmits the lubricating, integrating, accelerating, and anticipating forces that make an economy run. When it stops working, the credit market becomes the perfect obstacle, transmitting paralysis throughout the system, dislocating the flows of exchange, and choking off everything that has grown dependent on it.

Expressed as a number, a debt makes economic sense only when the amount of borrowing is set against some other quantity, such as the amount of collateral or the borrower's prospects for future earnings. For example, to hear that someone wants a $1 million home mortgage tells us very little: it matters greatly whether the house is worth $1 million or $3 million, and whether the borrower has an annual income of $30,000 or $300,000. That is to say, it matters to the lender if the house is worth more than the loan, and it matters to the borrower if there is enough income to pay the interest, if not the principal. Either way, that $1 million mortgage will look radically different if the value of the house drops or the income disappears, or both—as millions have recently learned to their dismay. From this scenario we can draw a more general lesson: the functioning of any financial debt is grounded in its claim on some other source of value. At some point that is impossible to know in advance, any debt can be cut off from the values, properties, and capacities that secured it, whether that may be some physical object, another paper asset, or a debtor's ability to produce. At that point, a debt ceases to function as a merely financial arrangement and takes on a new range of possible meanings: at one extreme it can be effectively *infinite*—an impossible demand that continues to control people without any prospect of release—or at the other extreme it may be effectively *void*—an empty command that will disappear like a wisp of smoke in the face of a determined act of refusal. Recent events have provided millions of people with indelible experiences of these volatile extremes: what appears at one moment as a simple quantity can quickly become crushingly immense or totally insubstantial. To put it in the most general terms: a system of debt both *allows* and *requires* people to build upon the void without being crushed by the infinite.

What are the salient features and tendencies of the neoliberal regime of indebtedness? Here are some general indicators and significant examples:

—In principle, public debt can operate as an instrument of collective rationality, a mechanism through which political power claims the economic resources it needs to enact its decisions. In current practice, however, it works the opposite way: as a mechanism through which the costs of collective irrationality—rampant greed and recklessness, exorbitant externalities, perverse incentives, and systemic dangers—are imposed on everybody. We face something more enveloping than the classic contradiction between the privatization of profits and the socialization of risks: public debt has shouldered the burden of sustaining an economic system whose leaders and ideologues have consistently repudiated the very idea of public responsibility.

—Business debt, both financial and nonfinancial, has moved far beyond its older functions in trade and investment. The overriding goal of neoliberal policy has been to unleash the powers of financialization, whether through outright deregulation or state-backed enterprises and partnerships. This effort has focused fundamentally on the expansion of techniques for organizing and marketing debt, so that any company can engage in financial engineering while the state conjures away the constraints of moral hazard and social responsibility. The devices have become infamous: the general category of derivative contracts, the securitization or pseudo-validation of unsecured value, credit default swaps, and collateralized debt obligations, as well as the whole arsenal of the leveraged buyout crews. Time and again, the collapse of entities created by financial "innovation"—from savings and loans to hedge funds to private equity firms—has led to public bailouts at enormous expense.

—Household debt has changed most dramatically, led by the United States. In the postwar period, and especially since the 1970s, whole new categories have emerged, led by ever fancier forms of mortgage financing and home equity loans. But there are also growing portions of debt that have been rendered necessary because formerly public provisions (such as education) must now be financed through personal debts. Where the protections of the social safety net have been stunted or rescinded, household debt will be required to mediate between the discipline of labor markets and the discipline of bankruptcy laws.

—Total debt levels are rising as the global economy requires more and more fiscal fuel to keep going. In the US, led by the financial and household sectors, the ratio between total debt and GDP reached 358 percent in 2008. Of course, there is no automatic feedback loop between increased debt and greater prosperity; on the contrary, for decades the richest countries have taken on larger ratios of debt while experiencing slower growth rates in return.[28] As we saw in the previous chapter, greater levels of debt have boosted overall demand in the face of stagnation, propping up an increasingly unsustainable economic structure. And now it appears that another expansion of debt will be required to cushion the effects of the collapse: a double bind of indebtedness.

—Government debt in the G7 countries, even in the wake of safety-net shredding, continues to grow, especially in the US and the UK. Although the EU as a whole moderated its growth up until the brink of the financial crisis, it will not remain immune to the pressure. Stimulus spending and bailouts will undo whatever prudence had accomplished before, as the threat of fiscal insolvency hangs in the air. Again we can notice the cruel effects of the historical double whammy: having paid the overhead costs for neoliberal restructuring and deregulation, taxpayers and workers will now pay again to repair the wreckage.

28   Robert Pollin, *Contours of Descent: US Economic Fractures and the Landscape of Global Austerity* (London: Verso, 2003), p. 132 ff.

—Nonfinancial corporate debt continues to careen through its own booms and busts. During the lead-up to the meltdown, many companies were still following the eighties and nineties playbook by financing mergers and acquisitions, expanding into financial operations, and relying more heavily on credit lines. One of the biggest bubbles of all surrounded commercial real estate, which sucked up oceans of investment and turned them into skyscrapers and business parks. The result was a massive overaccumulation in all forms, and, later, the resulting shakeout. (We reviewed Robert Brenner's argument about this pattern in the previous chapter.) Meanwhile, of course, financial sector debt had been ballooning for decades, until virtually the whole sector leveraged itself high into thin air, far beyond its ability to believe in its own fabrications. The 2008–09 crash was the first in what is likely to be a long series of debt destructions, mitigated by bailouts funded by public debt.

—In the US, the UK, and the EU, the ratio of household debt to GDP has been rising alarmingly since the 1980s. Even so, these broad measures conceal the very differences that the wealth and inequality figures revealed: debt means rather different things for households at different ends of the scale. For wealthier households, more debt is associated with greater ability to borrow for houses, durable goods, education, and so on. For everybody else, increased debt should be seen in the context of the persistent stagnation in wages, where borrowing against a house became the easiest and perhaps the only way to support consumption. In either case, those who took on debt in the form of mortgages and home equity loans are now seeing their equity flowing back to the financial institutions. And people will find themselves even more vulnerable in the downturn. (In 2007, household debt as a percentage of disposable income topped 130 percent in the US; the EU ratio was about 90 percent.)

—China's government debt has totaled around 20 percent of GDP in recent years, a fraction of the proportion seen elsewhere, and a fraction of the savings and reserves the country has built up over decades of export growth.

— In developing countries, the official agencies concentrate on the ratio of the cost of external debt service to GDP. Contrary to the image of constantly mounting debt burdens across the developing world, this ratio fluctuates in both directions. Between 1990 and 2005, for example, some economies (Chile, Malaysia) have seen a reduction, while others have seen a rise (Mexico, Hungary, Thailand), but in very few cases does the ratio reach above 10 percent. (The extremes are instructive: as of 2005, China's ratio was 1.2 percent, Vietnam's was 1.8 percent, Turkey's 11.6 percent, and Belize's 20.7 percent.) Overall, the burden of debt service is rising in middle-income countries but dropping in low-income countries. According to the World Bank, the total debt service for middle- and low-income countries reached 5.1 percent of their total GDP in 2005; such countries are now net exporters of capital to the rich countries. Finally, in poorer countries, public sector debt has been drying up while the expansion of private sector finance has been notably rocky, vulnerable to even the gentlest crises in the global markets.

Everywhere, the regime of indebtedness continues to expand and intensify, crossing systemic limits hitherto untested by neoliberal calculations. As it expands and deepens, it redraws the inner divisions and outer boundaries of every social body. Through its operations the scission between wealth and poverty turns into a self-reinforcing pincer. On one side, wherever there is great wealth there will have been what Harvey calls "accumulation by dispossession" or, more simply, "enclosure." This means something more than the privatization of profits generated by public resources, although that has been a fundamental mechanism throughout the history of capitalism. Enclosure entails the privatization of everything—the appropriation of all goods and resources that might once have been held in common, "[land], water, the fruits of the forest, the spaces of custom and communal negotiation, the mineral substrate, the life of rivers and oceans, the very airwaves . . ."[29] Instead of focusing strictly on the dramatic extremes of the rich and the poor, we should examine the relationship between those who own and those who owe. On the other side, "exposure" likewise means something more than the socialization of risks whereby private enterprises are underwritten by public funds: today exposure puts everybody at the risk of irreparable loss, whether the system functions or not. Whether it is a matter of opening labor or commodity markets to international competition or cutting public provision in the name of market discipline, the regime of indebtedness demands an expansion of compulsory responsibilities and punitive obligations. Whether this pincer of indebtedness leads to further rounds of enclosure and exposure, and thus a deepening of domestic and global expropriation and impoverishment, or whether it sparks new political demands—grounded in an awareness that our collective indebtedness can be organized on wholly different terms—remains to be seen.

In any case, it is clear that a politics of the crisis that seeks to construct solidarity out of indebtedness will look very different from reforms that invoke the principles of equality and freedom alone. Even if some governments address domestic inequality in the name of greater democratic participation, and even if poverty reduction programs bring an improvement in local living standards—and neither outcome can be assumed because neither strategy ranks high on any official list of priorities—the implacable apparatuses of accumulation will still stand. Only a politics of the indebted can carry through the transformative possibilities of the crisis, locating

---

29   Retort, *Afflicted Powers: Capital and Spectacle in a New Age of War* (London: Verso, 2005) pp. 193–4.

sources of solidarity in the midst of the terrible collective punishments inflicted by the precipitous collapse and desperate restoration of the prevailing regime of indebtedness.

Meanwhile, as reform plans are debated and solemn resolutions passed, the whole setup that makes a few so rich and most others so poor, both within each country and across the world system, continues to do its work without waiting for reasons or excuses.

3   The Economic Consequences
of the Perpetual Peace

One must know that war is common, strife is justice, and that all things come to pass by strife and necessity.

—Heraclitus, Fragment 80

"One must know that war is common—" Heraclitus starts to say. "You should know—" "One must realize—" "*Il faut connaître—*" "*Man soll aber wissen—*" The fragment begins by interrupting and insisting. A disagreement is already under way, the conflict has already begun. We can hear that Heraclitus is arguing with someone (maybe Homer), although it sounds as if he is also arguing with himself. The words themselves struggle to define each other in the course of the fragment, one term pinning another before being cast down in its turn, a string of equations unable to strike a balance. Not even this declaration is exempt from the strife of which it speaks. That is why it has always sounded so aggressive and uncertain: it provokes not only those who might have wished that the world would someday be at peace, but also those who hoped that our wisdom might make it so. Heraclitus argues otherwise. You must learn, he insists, that nothing happens without a struggle, and that knowledge takes part—and takes sides—in every battle. Neither exalted ideals nor finely turned figures of speech can settle our differences. Or, to put it another way: whenever you think you've found peace on earth, look out for the battle raging just around the corner, because you're part of it, too.

This lesson seems especially apt for the good citizens of the West, many of whom tend to mistake their own moments of private repose for the final realization of peace on earth. Against those who assume that the planet has been working its way toward an eventual state of tranquil prosperity—except for some final pieces of humanitarian business to be tidied up, a few cases of unresolved ethnic unrest, some shocking atrocities, and an occasional multi-national police action—one should point out that the fault lines of conflict keep spreading all over the place. The front lines of warfare may not be visible all at once, but they cut everywhere, across households and workplaces, down streets and over countrysides, around patches of urban turf and rural tracts, through overlapping jurisdictions and spheres of influence; they weave back and forth through forced migrations and acts of exodus, erased and overwritten by territorial seizures, armed threats, surgical strikes, and grand strategic zones. What was advertised as an era of peace, when war was finally confined to the hinterlands or carefully administered in calibrated doses, should instead be recognized as a generalized system of violence long in the making, a fraught world where peace remains a precarious and elusive exception—and that only by virtue of careful stagecraft. In the name of keeping the global peace, the strongest combatants have claimed permanent emergency powers with monopoly privileges.

So what else is new, someone might ask. Perhaps every social order simmers with unresolvable conflict. Perhaps the borderline between peace and warfare cannot be settled precisely because it delimits and justifies the social order itself—all politics begins by drawing the line that casts out "enemies" and circumscribes the place where "friends" must adjudicate their own differences. If that's the case, peacemakers can never expect to establish a final settlement of any conflict; they can only try to regulate and sanction particular strategies for deal-ing with the unceasing strife that makes the world what it is. Indeed, a declaration of peace, even more than a declaration of war, can be pronounced and enforced only by the most powerful combatants, inasmuch as peacekeeping requires extensive control over territories and populations. Citing such reasons, certain philosophers have for centuries tried to disabuse people of their longings for a lasting peace, since it could be achieved only through the greatest tyranny. In recent years, the argument has been boiled down further: now we're told that the desire for peace itself, like any Utopian aspiration, is tyrannical to the core. Get used to it, we hear; history never rests and it always spells trouble.

Is that so? Does history, as opposed to philosophy, really demonstrate the impossibility of peace? The latest balance sheets do not look good. Historians have ventured the observation that the world enjoyed only two or three years of general peace during the entire twentieth century. (Those precious few months, it seems, slipped by somewhere during the late 1920s.[1]) When it comes to the conduct of war, modern societies have been tirelessly enterprising. The techniques of slaughter long ago outstripped all strategic objectives. At the same time, the pursuit of strategic objectives now penetrates every dimension of social life, from the largest collectivities to the most intimate relationships. Every war starts at home. One can speak without metaphor of the "arming" and "armoring" of subjectivity, of tactical cunning in daily life, of constant training and battle-readiness to compete over everything that can be fought for. This perpetual striving and scheming, coupled with a deeply instilled defensiveness, has become the elemental condition of contemporary subjectivity: the armoring consists precisely in refusing to acknowledge that the will to succeed, elevated to the status of a social ideal, knows no boundaries. When people speak of *homo economicus* as the default mode of subjectivity, they affirm that a diffuse kind of war has been permanently installed in the social life of humankind. But the competitive urge has nothing to do with the so-called state

---

1   Eric Hobsbawm, *The Age of Extremes* (New York: Vintage, 1996), p. 13.

of nature: everyday aggressiveness has become the subtle, advanced attitude of civilized people, exhausted by their sublimations and eager to claim their spoils before the whole setup falls apart.[2] The idea that people should work and sacrifice together in a time of war has been overturned: just the opposite, an endless war will seem worth fighting only when it makes possible new schemes of enrichment and new rounds of consumption.

It is often said that the conduct of war has undergone one qualitative leap after another, from 1914 (total war), to 1939 (blitzkrieg), 1945 (Hiroshima), and so on all the way to the "surgically" efficient Gulf War, which was so well staged for its Western audiences that it "did not take place" as a recognizable historical event at all, as Jean Baudrillard famously declared.[3] The best confirmation of Baudrillard's thesis is the fact that the US/UK military and economic "containment" of Iraq after 1991 was never registered as a war by the Western media, despite frequent bombings and extensive civilian casualties. In that sense, the Gulf War did not take place, and it has never stopped not taking place. The question of whether "economic sanctions" should count as a kind of warfare has not been pursued very far in public discussions—not because it seems to be such a marginal aspect of war, but because it speaks too plainly of the ordinary brutal aspects of the current economic system. On the other hand, the major killing contests of recent decades—think of Rwanda, Sierra Leone, Chechnya—"did not take place" in another sense, becoming famous belatedly as global catastrophes without having been matters of global public concern in the first place. Without a sense of the systemic causes of such events, the spectacle of violence in distant lands serves mainly

---

2   On the possibilities of "disarming" the cynical subject, see Peter Sloterdijk, *Critique of Cynical Reason,* trans. Michael Eldred (Minneapolis: University of Minnesota Press, 1987), p. 379.

3   Jean Baudrillard, *The Gulf War Did Not Take Place,* trans. Paul Patton (Bloomington: Indiana University Press, 1995).

to impress us with our own passivity. The key lesson we can draw from these experiences is therefore negative: that so much killing can go on in so many places, onscreen and off, without being recognized as a generalized system of violence is indeed a fundamental historical event.

During the 1990s and early 2000s, there were somewhere between fifty and sixty-six wars raging at any given time, usually "civil wars" but also including conflicts that were "world wars" in all but name (the Gulf War, the Balkans, the Congo).[4] That statistic scrupulously counts only acts of hostility between two or more organized forces, but our era is perhaps most notable for the proliferation of quasi-permanent warlike situations that do not fit that definition: think of the land-mined landscapes, free-range armed gangs, surrogate and private armies, police-and-prison industrial complexes, apartheid regimes, cleansing campaigns, military blockades, and of course the promiscuous risks posed by weapons of mass destruction (whether nuclear, biochemical, or conventional). The range of dangers is both unevenly distributed and comprehensively planetary at the same time. More to the point, the official reports inform us that wars "occur disproportionately in poor countries" and that 90 percent of war dead are non-combatants. No matter how a war is defined, it continues to be true that the dead, debilitated, and missing are most likely to be poor people, whether drafted as fighters or targeted as obstacles. Those who fight and those who flee as refugees become as invisible as those who are simply wiped from the map. That is one way to understand the "globalization" of warfare: the exercise of social violence has become effectively indifferent to the limits of state power and civil order, taking aim at everybody or nobody in turn. (Étienne Balibar has spoken of this situation in terms of "extreme violence," in which the world comes to be divided between

---

4   World Bank, *World Development Report 2000/2001: Attacking Poverty* (Washington, D.C.: World Bank, 2000), p. 50.

"life zones" and "death zones."[5]) Yet even the most immediate acts of violence are nevertheless mediated, transformed into images for wider transmission. People are killed "to send a message": some die as disposable "nobodies," disappearing in the night; others die as sacrificial "everybodies" in well-publicized cataclysms. This stylized conversation of killing has become a standard feature of the daily news, but it is not always clear who is sending the message, or to whom, or what it is supposed to mean: raised to the level of a global dialogue between states, faiths, or "civilizations," the exercise of violence is the only language that becomes more incomprehensible the more often it is used. That is why television acts as an essential supplement to the worldwide organization of war: the TV screen, in occasionally showing the faces of a few victims, serves as a bulletin board for all killers, large and small, to post their threats for maximum diffusion. It is where threats become threats; that is, where a sense of being endangered is turned into a promise to attack, ad infinitum. Television announces that the fatal messages have been sent even when the purported senders and recipients can't hear, won't hear, or have already perished.

Perhaps the crucial technological breakthroughs in the conduct of warfare do not involve military hardware—as impressive as that is—but rather the telecommunications systems that make war more or less "actual" to its planners, combatants, victims, and audiences. The distances between those who decide strategy, those who fight, those who die, and those who sit and watch are becoming more manipulable and more incommensurable. As the techniques of projecting physical violence expand, so, too, do the means of channeling its psychic and symbolic force. To put it simply: every military strategy requires a media strategy (and vice versa). In an

---

5   Étienne Balibar, "Outline of a Topography of Cruelty: Citizenship and Civility in the Era of Global Violence," in *We, the People of Europe?: Reflections on Transnational Citizenship*, trans. James Swenson, (Princeton: Princeton University Press, 2004), pp. 115–32.

obvious way, warfare has always needed a "media strategy" to bind together a people and its allies as a fighting force, and on the other side to identify and undermine the enemy. But media strategies, like culture itself, do not operate along a single front: they involve all kinds of back-and-forth movements, stitching productive forces and legal institutions to group identities and libidinal drives. They are not limited to the background processes of motivation or persuasion; strategies do not merely organize what is already there. Social bodies of all kinds are constituted and contested strategically, as practical dispositions of material force and more or less effective instruments of attack and defense. That is the crucial political point: media strategies now perform constitutional functions *in absentia*, producing "legitimation" without recourse to legal processes, a "popular mandate" without recourse to democratic procedures, and "universal principles" that need not last beyond the particular task at hand.

In such a situation, it is less and less clear how military power of any kind relates to the political constituencies, economic interests, or human values it is supposed to represent and enforce. Or, to put it the other way around, it is all too easy to see how media strategies become essential when the distinctions between friend and enemy have become structurally unstable or fungible, and when advanced military technology cannot help but inflict surplus casualties and collateral damage. In the constant chattering about potential enemies, we always hear an insistence on the difference between a people and its leadership, or between an important trading partner and its unfriendly government, as if such distinctions could purchase forgiveness in advance from innocent victims, even in the act of threatening their lives. And as we have seen repeatedly in the United States, televised discussions about establishing "public support" for military action are not really the political precondition for going to war, but the clearest sign that the media strategies of war have already started. Not only is it unnecessary to build a "domestic consensus" for starting a war, but it also turns out to be impossible to reach an "international consensus" that there is a war going on. (Likewise, a domestic consensus to end a war does not mean that an end is anywhere in sight, and an international consensus against aggression can be brushed aside with a shrug.) Today, a war can be packaged in all kinds of ways, as a spectacular miniseries or wrapped up in a blanket of euphemism and censorship; some are built up in anticipation, through a long-term marketing campaign, while others barely become news long after the worst has passed. Round-the-clock panic stimulation or willful ignorance: these are the twin poles of the world-picture offered by the media strategists. In this way the real stakes of the various ongoing conflicts are made unreadable, whether by exaggerating the lines of antagonism or by pretending that none exist.

The macroscopic evidence points to an unsettling conclusion: what might appear to be a growing confusion between peace and war—in which the traditional distinctions no longer seem to fit the facts on the ground—should really be seen as the default program and policy of the major powers. The constant invocation of generalized peace neatly inverts the spread of violence and vulnerability into every layer of social life. Debates about the relative wisdom of this or that police action typically proceed from an unexamined ratification of a larger historical process, namely, the emergence of a US-led neoliberal capitalism, or Empire, pursuing a ferocious new logic of control that requires the pacification of populations and the management of permanently unstable and uneven development. After spending the 1990s marveling at the triumphalism of capital as it careened through booms and busts without losing its missionary zeal, and spending the first decade of the 2000s watching blockbuster invasions alternate with lethal stalemates, it is time for us to ask how the market system advances and defends itself by military force across a global battlefield, spurring belligerent rivalries over resources, the fortification of borders and supply routes, and indeed a new round of aggressive austerity programs, hostile "structural adjustment" schemes, and genuinely bloody acts of "creative destruction."

A long history could be told here concerning the expansion of warfare and the pursuit of expanding markets over the past 200 years or so, in spite of every claim that one is the complete opposite of the other. At the present moment, we are standing at a remarkable juncture of this history. We have just witnessed yet another attempt to corner the market in violence and to monopolize its legitimacy in the hands of a single superstate. Although that attempt—which includes not only the campaigns in Iraq and Afghanistan, but also the assertion of NATO beyond Europe and the spread of more than 700 US military bases around the world—has proved to be far from invincible, it has nevertheless succeeded in fundamental ways. The superstate strategy remains, at least for now, the only available framework to provide security for the global markets. In terms of US politics, this means recognizing the fundamental continuities from Clinton to Bush Jr. to Obama—whether haggling in Doha, spreading shock and awe over Baghdad, or summiting with the G20 in Toronto. Indeed it would be possible to trace the story further back: even during the Cold War, the West began supplementing its strategy of deterrence with a long-term market strategy aimed at training socialist and third world countries in the intricate discipline of indebtedness. From that point on, nuclear strategy and market strategy complemented each other well: both laid claim to the future of the whole planet, replacing absolute danger with finely wrought negotiations between the unsustainable and the unsurvivable.

From a broader historical perspective, however, it has become possible to ask if the interstate settlement that has structured the political dimension of global governance since World War II is now coming apart. Within the milieu of mainstream policy debate, Philip Bobbitt has argued forcefully for the emergence of a sweepingly new dispensation: not simply some shift in the balance between market institutions and nation-states, but the thoroughgoing transformation of both into a historically original system of "market-states." In Bobbitt's account, presented in *The Shield of Achilles* (2002) and *Terror and Consent* (2008), the coming society of market-states will encompass a variety of models, accommodating German and Japanese variations, but the United States will be uniquely qualified to lead the overall system, owing to its open-ended constitutional order and its morally guided military power.[6] The inauguration of the world of market-states will bring to an end the era of modern states, whose centuries-long evolution reached its terminus with the end of the East/West division in 1990.[7] In the earlier book, written largely before 9/11, the establishment of the era of the market-state seemed a stormy but optimistic process. The United States had weathered the challenges of the twentieth century with its moral vision and constitutional order intact, and now stood ready to sponsor the construction of a new system based on its model of democracy. By the time of the later book, the nascent order seems much more fraught with peril. The United States, as the only power capable of deciding upon a global strategy, must now fight dissent, backsliding, and terror at every turn. There is no reason to doubt that the violence employed to establish an order of market-states will be more than matched by the violence employed to defend it. As states shift their focus away from such old-fashioned goals as social welfare or domestic self-sufficiency and toward the paramount goal of clearing the ground for private enterprise, it becomes easy to imagine that the most drastic forms

---

6   Philip Bobbitt, *The Shield of Achilles: War, Peace, and the Course of History* (New York: Knopf, 2002); *Terror and Consent: The Wars for the Twenty-first Century* (New York: Anchor, 2009 [first edition 2008]). Henceforth cited as SA and TC, respectively.
7   For a thorough critique of the historical lineages and projections of *The Shield of Achilles*, see Gopal Balakrishnan, "Algorithms of War," *New Left Review* 23 (September/October 2003), pp. 5–33. Reprinted in *Antagonistics: Capitalism and Power in an Age of War* (London: Verso, 2009).

of market fundamentalism still lie ahead, to be imposed not by political choice but under the cover of irrevocable austerity plans, backed by full police power.

In light of Bobbitt's scenario (and his hypothesis of an epochal shift finds echoes throughout contemporary debates) we can distinguish three ways in which the state's monopoly of violence grounds itself in a regime of indebtedness.

The oldest and most familiar connection between war and debt revolves around the state's need to tax and borrow in order to fight. Every state enlists its people as combatants by imposing the costs of war upon them, whether directly, through the conscription of bodies and property, or indirectly, through increasingly complex means of financing. It is worth remembering that Immanuel Kant, in his 1795 essay "Perpetual Peace," argued that the "power of money" [*Geldmacht*] is the "most reliable instrument of war," more dependable than armies or alliances. He warned that the ability of the state to accumulate wealth, like the capacity to maintain a standing army, functions as an immediate threat to neighboring states. Likewise, Kant saw that a credit system could be used as an "instrument of aggression" by allowing a state to amass armed forces well beyond its immediate resources, thereby giving it an advantage over more fiscally prudent neighbors. As part of his proposal to establish peace, then, Kant wanted to prohibit foreign debts and to limit the ability of any state to build an army through mercenary means.[8] As a result of such strictures, the power of money will serve "the noble cause of peace" by nourishing in each state the "spirit of commerce" and thereby steering all nations toward mutually beneficial cooperation, securely bound by trade.[9] Although he supposed this tendency toward commercial harmony

---

8   Immanuel Kant, "Perpetual Peace," in *Political Writings*, ed. by Hans Reiss and trans. by H.B. Nisbet (Cambridge: Cambridge University Press, 1991), pp. 94–5. For the original text, see *Zum ewigen Frieden* (Stuttgart: Reclam, 1984), pp. 5–6.

9   Kant, "Perpetual Peace," p. 114. (German edition, p. 33).

to be guaranteed by natural inclinations, Kant declared that we also have a duty to bring it about, a universal moral obligation to promote peace through trade and thus supplant the merely private or national debts that promote war.

The second link between war and debt is really just the obverse of the first: alongside debts imposed in order to make war, there are debts imposed in order to keep the peace. Or to put it more simply: there are debts of the winners and debts of the losers. Perhaps it is more accurate to describe the debts of the defeated as a tribute, or protection money, paid as part of the spoils of war. Just as Kant wanted to tame the "warlike inclinations" of the modern state by blocking its ability to put itself in debt, John Maynard Keynes, in his 1919 book *The Economic Consequences of the Peace*, wanted to warn against the dangers of inflicting punitive reparations upon the losing side. His condemnation of the economic provisions of the Versailles Treaty is uncompromising: the Allies aimed to skin Germany alive "year by year in perpetuity" in what he thought would be judged "one of the most outrageous acts of a cruel victor in civilized history."[10] Instead of a crippling collective punishment carried out by economic experts, Keynes insisted, a different kind of peace must be envisioned, one that acknowledged that the world had already been unified as a single market, so that treating one's trading partners as enemies could not help but diminish one's own prosperity as well.[11] For Keynes as for Kant, the best prospects for peace lay in the growth of a global economy where each nation helped all the others by keeping its own economic house in order. That is as far as the liberal imagination has ever wanted to go: a cosmopolitan capitalism, selfish on principle at home while demanding access and hospitality abroad.

Even those modest hopes remain unfulfilled. Having conspicuously failed to abolish foreign debts, standing armies, and the use

---

10   John Maynard Keynes, *The Economic Consequences of the Peace* (New York: Penguin Books, 1995), p. 168.

11   *Ibid.*, p. 295.

of debt as a weapon in international conflicts, the capitalist system continues to generate destabilizing disparities between military and market power. In Bobbitt's vision of the market-state, such tensions must be embraced rather than ignored. Instead of worrying about the incompatibility between disproportionate military power and a decentered economic system entrusted with keeping the peace, we are supposed to imagine the emergence of a new kind of nonterritorial sovereignty capable of reconciling individual interests and global strategy without falling back upon state-based institutions. The rule of law will now be dedicated to a variety of tasks that no longer presume the equality of nations or peoples: first, to secure the exceptional status of US power; second, to safeguard the transmission mechanisms of capital (especially in ensuring maximum mobility of property rights and the convertibility of currencies); and third, to provide an atmosphere of "opportunity" to private individuals. The looming transition to a new order nevertheless poses a major problem. Once the legal and political functions of the state-form are outsourced to corporations, devolved to local groups, or assigned to as-yet-unbuilt global institutions, how will it be possible to enforce the dictates of the system?

Bobbitt is clearly preoccupied by this question, and he devotes much effort to reformulating the notions of "consent" and "legitimacy" in suitably updated terms. But it is hard to avoid the impression that these values, wholly bestowed by media strategies, have been reduced to a spectral tautology: consent confers legitimacy upon whatever power can produce the appearance of consent. Perhaps the notion of "consent" makes more sense when it is pronounced "obligation," deflecting the subjective orientation from the political realm (with its vestigial symbolic rituals, parties, etc.) to the economic realm (where it signifies a prior agreement to abide by the rules of exchange). In relieving people of their outmoded obligations to defective political entities, the market-state offers them the unlimited obligation to compete, on a world scale, for the mere chance to live. Everyone will welcome this liberation, we are told, except for the terrorists, who will ungratefully take advantage of the freedoms offered by market-states to disrupt the flows of commerce and defy the authority of the global police.

A rhetorical/ideological bifurcation runs through this program: on one hand, the need to insist on an authority that can secure the system at a universal level, ensuring that no local defections or oppositions can trouble its supremacy; on the other hand, the need to appeal to diversely composed constituencies in a different universal key, emphasizing the individual advantages of accepting the insecurities of market competition. The media strategies described earlier can now be recognized as the crucial hinges whereby spectators find themselves inserted into the great war of the age: the fight to maintain the dominion of the market-state against its opponents—a category that includes those who refuse to surrender the prerogatives of nation-states as well as those who refuse the state or the system as such. A third kind of indebtedness emerges here. All of those who want to picture themselves as the free agents and entrepreneurs of the market-state must agree in advance to pay whatever it costs to remake the world as an arena of opportunity. In effect, such liabilities are unconditional and inexhaustible, because they must cover not only the expense of fighting endless wars but also of buying off or fencing in all of those who have been left out of the deal.

In order to get a sense of the way military and media strategies present a united front, we can turn to two recent US National Security Strategy (NSS) documents, one issued by the Bush Jr. administration in September 2002 and the other by the Obama administration in May 2010. The production of these documents has been mandated by Congress since 1986 as part of the annual budget process, but in practice security strategies have been issued only sporadically by recent administrations. (There have been nine, starting with Reagan: '87, '88, '90, '91, '93, '94, '97, '99, '02, '06, and now '10).[12] Although the ostensible purpose of these documents is to support specific budget priorities, they have evolved into stylized statements of doctrine, setting forth an official explanation of the relationship between armed force, economic organization, and global order. Each version of the text deploys a weaponized rhetoric through which the messy realities of imperial rule have been processed into something resembling a corporate prospectus. To the cynical observer, it may be surprising that there is any explanation of official violence at all: as Donald Rumsfeld was fond of saying, it is what it is. But it seems just as obvious that the NSS is not addressed to any political community that could or would offer legitimation and consent in response. Instead it should be read as a necessarily mixed message aimed at a varied audience encompassing allies and competitors, friends and enemies. As we will see, each text cannot help but present a contradictory and even incoherent ideological performance, and in this way each serves as an exemplary instance of the way media discourse and market logic overdetermine the exercise of US power.

The 2002 NSS became famous as George W. Bush's sweeping declaration of unilateralism; the 2010 NSS has been greeted as Obama's reversal, even repudiation, of the former administration's stance. It is too simple to treat them as opposites, just as it is too

---

12 The second Bush NSS, in 2006, is organized around the same headings as the 2002 report; indeed, it resembles a kind of progress report, revisiting the goals of 2002 and claiming, over and over, "Mission accomplished." There is one wholly new section headed "Globalization," but it is not at all concerned with the free trade gospel reiterated earlier. It deals instead with illicit trade, AIDS, and environmental disasters—as if the Bush administration registered the phenomenon of globalization only through its more dire consequences. This awkward inclusion could be read as a sign of the unresolved contradiction between the market and military rhetorics deployed throughout the document. Of course, the 1999 Clinton NSS sounds quite a bit like an early rehearsal for the Bush and Obama documents. It is organized around the three themes of "enhanced security," "bolstering economic prosperity," and "promoting democracy and human rights."

simple to treat them as a straightforward continuity. (On the ground, Obama has not reversed Bush at all, as Tariq Ali has demonstrated with devastating clarity.[13]) At the rhetorical/ideological level, the two texts are paradoxically complementary. The Bush text presents us with an aggressive posture we are meant to recognize as a real threat, even if it is couched in the standard terms of ideals, rights, etc., none of which we can really be expected to believe. The Obama text gives us essentially the same grandiose boilerplate and asks us to take it at its word, while downplaying the militarist posturing as a pro forma distraction. Both documents are written in the hammered and buffed prose of speechwriters, which faithfully reproduces the partisan phrases while cleaving to an invariant core of all-conquering optimism that would not be out of place in a Coca-Cola or Merrill Lynch commercial.

The 2002 NSS is a fairly brief text, just thirty-one pages long, including a three-page preface over Bush's signature.[14] It rides from grandiose highs to cautious lows and back again, opening with a celebration of the "unprecedented—and unequaled—strength and influence" of the United States, and an invocation of "human dignity" (sections I and II); rehearsing the threats of global terrorism, regional conflicts, and weapons of mass destruction (sections III–V); answering those threats with the promise of global free trade, the virtuous circle of development, and cooperation among the major powers (sections VI–VIII). Coming full circle, the document finally closes with an explicit affirmation of "American military

13   Tariq Ali, "President of Cant," *New Left Review* 61 (January/February 2010), pp. 99–116. See also "Social Work with Guns," Andrew Bacevich, *London Review of Books*, December 17, 2009, pp. 7–8. The evidence keeps mounting. Just a week before the 2010 NSS was released, it was reported that the Obama administration had authorized "a broad expansion of clandestine military activity" across the Middle East, Central Asia, and the Horn of Africa, aiming "to make such efforts more systematic and long term." (Mark Mazetti, "U.S. Is Said to Expand Secret Actions in Mideast," *New York Times*, May 24, 2010.)

14   White House, *National Security Strategy of the United States* (2002 edition). Originally available online: whitehouse.gov; accessed October 12, 2002.

strength" and plans to expand US presence around the world. The very last lines ground these plans in a quasi-theological claim about the connection between market dynamism and military strength: "A diverse, modern society has inherent, ambitious, entrepreneurial energy. Our strength comes from what we do with that energy. That is where our national security begins."[15] The document ends at the threshold where economic power is transformed into imperial power: although every "modern" society may possess entrepreneurial energy (this is the moral basis for the global economy), the US uses its energy to create a transcendent strength. The very force that is supposed to bind all nations together somehow makes the US uniquely dominant.

When the Bush White House released its first NSS on September 20, 2002, eight days after President Bush addressed the UN on the subject of challenging Iraq, *The Economist* called it "one of the most important geopolitical documents produced for a long time," even though it "puts forward no new foreign-policy ideology."[16] That sounds paradoxical, but it is accurate. The 2002 NSS was important, in other words, not because it changed the course of US policy but because it reset the terms of its public presentation. To be more precise, it was important because it articulated a contradiction between economic and military priorities, collapsing the gap (inherited from Clinton) between neoliberal market strategies and neoconservative superpower posturing. Why, then, were large portions of the "Bush doctrine" indistinguishable from similar documents issued by Clinton? Was the headline-grabbing innovation—the explicit claim of the right to preemptive military strikes—really anything new? And why, if the White House had already decided upon its main military strategy in 2002, did it feel any need to put forth justifications? Rather than dismissing the whole circus

---

15   NSS 2002, p. 31.
16   "Unprecedented Power, Colliding Ambitions," *The Economist*, September 26, 2002, p. 27.

of UN meetings and fabricated evidence as "just for show," it would be better to approach the issue from the other side: why did they have to put on a show at all? If the only arena in which "moral and legal" justifications can be adjudicated is a "public sphere" emptied of all effective mechanisms of answerability and disconnected from democratic forms of counterpower, why did the Bush administration play the game of keeping up appearances? Why would such a power want or need to present itself as justified, let alone civilized? In the eyes of whom?

As the radical group Retort has described the situation after 9/11:

States can behave like maddened beasts . . . and still get their way. They regularly do. But the present madness is singular: the dimension of spectacle has never before interfered so palpably, so insistently, with the business of keeping one's satrapies in order. And never before have spectacular politics been conducted in the shadow—the "historical knowledge"—of *defeat*. It remains to be seen what new mutation of the military-industrial-entertainment complex emerges from the shambles.[17]

In this light, one can see a bright thread of unhinged arrogance running through the 2002 NSS. Its invocations of pervasive risk mark precisely where imaginary imperatives organize strategic thinking. (Once again, battlefield commanders and bond traders speak the same tongue.) In fact, the NSS never spells out any reasons *against* using force, and it outlines a comprehensive range of reasons to justify doing so—encompassing specific threats, emerging threats, and the unspecified hostile behavior of "enemies of civilization." "The gravest danger," we are told, "lies at the crossroads of radicalism and technology," where "shadowy networks of individuals can

---

17   Retort, *Afflicted Powers: Capital and Spectacle in a New Age of War* (London: Verso, 2005), p. 37. The chapter "Permanent War" (pp. 78–107), and indeed the whole book, offers an indispensable account of the post-9/11 situation.

bring great chaos and suffering to our shores for less than it costs to purchase a single tank." Beyond this banner threat, a full array of dangers looms: from "other great powers," "strong states," "weak states," "failed states," and "the embittered few." "In the new world we have entered, the only path to peace and security is the path of action."[18]

Many commentators were struck by this sweeping threat to take action, which reached far beyond the particular claims concerning the need for a preemptive war with Iraq. In the circumstances, it seemed like a case of old-fashioned brinksmanship, warning "partisans of the deed" that the state itself can match their boldness and ferocity. In more concrete terms, the text proposes that American forces should now be retooled to support preemptive options, specifically by expanding intelligence operations and developing "rapid and precise" military capabilities. This certainly sounds like an ominous flexing of imperial muscle. Jürgen Habermas promptly argued that the NSS was a disturbing and "provocative document," and that its preemptive posture "brush[es] aside the civilizing achievements" of international law.[19] Of course the doctrine of preemptive strikes is hardly new—the Clinton-era documents had articulated it as well, and its practice surely extends as far back as you'd like to go—and one might wonder whether the very existence of nuclear weapons, for example, had not "brushed aside" the tentative accomplishments of international law long before, in spite of (or because of) all the treaties and conventions. So should we take Habermas's alarm seriously? Is he correct in asserting that this document, through simple performative force, can damage whatever progress has been made in "domesticating the state of nature among belligerent nations"? Does it take just one deliberate "slip of the tongue" to demonstrate that everything propping up the current global order—including respect for international law, political alliances, public opinion, and

---

18   NSS 2002, pp. iv–v.
19   Jürgen Habermas, "Letter to America," *The Nation*, December 16, 2002, p. 15.

fundamental rights—is actually up for grabs (and always was)? There is, in other words, a discursive "preemptive strike" enacted here, and its targets are clearly the historical allies of the US, the UN, and all domestic opposition. It consists in saying out loud, with solemn gravity, that the obligations of democratic procedure have already been satisfied, and therefore only those who affirm the administration's newly unlimited authority shall deserve its protection.

The 2010 NSS does indeed offer a change of tone. Reportedly drafted by Ben Rhodes, who also drafted Obama's December 2009 speech on the troop escalation in Afghanistan, the Prague speech on nuclear disarmament, the Cairo speech on the Muslim world, and the Nobel Peace Prize address, the text gathers threads from all of the president's major foreign policy pronouncements.[20] The document is organized by an enumeration of the components of American interests, tagged with the keywords "security," "prosperity," "values," and "international order." Each of these terms casts a more hard-edged shadow than the last: security depends on maintaining the US "military advantage" and reasserting US global leadership; prosperity depends on pushing the Washington blueprint for the international economy; the "values" in question are universal because they are American, rather than the other way around; and the international order will likewise turn on the US hub because the US alone sets the standard for democracy, human rights, and moral leadership.

Obama's list of threats to the US sounds remarkably like Bush's: they come from "nations, nonstate actors, and failed states." (That peculiar term, "nonstate actors," sounds less dangerous than the "shadowy networks of individuals" evoked earlier, but in its vagueness it actually includes more suspects.) Obama's threat list also

---

20   White House, *National Security Strategy of the United States* (2010 edition). Available online: whitehouse.gov. On Ben Rhodes, see Jason Horowitz, "Obama speechwriter Ben Rhodes is penning a different script for the world stage," *Washington Post*, January 12, 2010. Tariq Ali describes Obama's (and Rhodes's) style as a mixture of "sonorous banality and armour-plated hypocrisy" ("President of Cant," *NLR* 61, p. 115).

includes the problems of fuel dependence, environmental fragility, and "global criminal networks." In fact, globalization itself appears to be something of a threat here, intensifying "the dangers we face— from international terrorism and the spread of deadly technologies, to economic upheaval and a changing climate." In a text like this a comprehensive list of threats can cut two ways. On one hand, they promote a sense of besieged panic, against which the US appears to stand as the only solid opponent. On the other hand, the enumeration of dangers and challenges can sound like a jumble of disconnected problems that call for a series of disconnected, ad hoc solutions. Obama wants to avoid sounding fearful and paranoid because he would rather sound optimistic and keen to cooperate with others, but he does not concede any of the authority that his predecessor's fear-mongering style built into the presidency.

The usual distinctions between idealism and realism have no grip here. Starting from a "realist" and unprincipled stance on preemptive military action, the 2002 NSS claimed the authority to define and enforce its own principles of "human rights," which dovetails with the thoroughgoing neoliberal program of "pro-growth legal and regulatory policies" guided by the "moral principle" of free trade. (The document includes a ringing endorsement of the IMF's efforts to reform emerging economies and prevent financial crises— another piece of failed preemptive strategy.) Traveling the same terrain by a different route, Obama begins in the idealist register and works his way back to hard-nosed realism. As his phrases slip comfortably from "our interests" to "the interests we share with other nations and other peoples," it appears that nobody will be left out of the resurgent Pax Americana. Those who have tried to read the 2010 NSS for signs of a kinder and gentler stance on the projection of military power have turned immediately to a special section titled "Use of Force." Here we can read: "The United States must reserve the right to act unilaterally if necessary to defend our nation and our interests, yet we will also seek to adhere to standards that govern the use of force." That modest qualification about "standards" does not promise a change in current practice so much as a change in the way those practices are justified. Though legal and technical quibbles about the virtues of Guantánamo, unmanned drones, or the strangulation of Gaza may cause some consciences to twitch, an American president can always choose to take the absolute moral high ground. "Make no mistake," Obama intoned in his Nobel speech, "evil does exist in the world." With that remark, uttered while accepting an honor for a peace he has not made, Obama completed his collection of the rhetorical instruments of war.

As Bobbitt likes to put it, the current strategic function of the US is not "to make the world safe" but "to make the world available."[21] Again we are reminded of the "right of hospitality" recommended by Kant in "Perpetual Peace"—but rather than waiting to welcome seafarers, this will be a gunboat hospitality spreading its welcome everywhere. Each piece of friendly advice, each foreign aid package, every administrative security operation, each preemptive invasion can be coordinated under the rubric of spreading opportunity. We should note that the notion of "opportunity" is a major addition

---

21   Bobbitt, SA, p. 233. Niall Ferguson has also updated the Wilsonian phrase on behalf of an imperial America:

Far from retreating like some giant snail behind an electronic shell, the United States should be devoting a larger percentage of its vast resources to making the world safe for capitalism and democracy. This book has tried to show that, like free trade, these are not naturally occurring, but require strong institutional foundations of law and order. The proper role of an imperial America is to establish these institutions where they are lacking, if necessary—as in Germany and Japan—by military force.

Writing in 2001, Ferguson felt sure that the US would not rise to its imperial responsibilities. He concludes bitterly: "Perhaps that is the greatest disappointment facing the world in the twenty-first century: that the leaders of the one state with the economic resources to make the world a better place lack the guts to do it." As we will see in a later chapter, this rhetoric is remarkably similar to Bono's cajoling on behalf of development aid. Niall Ferguson, *The Cash Nexus: Money and Power in the Modern World, 1700–2000* (New York: Basic Books, 2001), p. 418.

to the ideological lexicon. (It appears thirty-four times in the 2010 NSS.) Somewhat more up-to-date than "democracy" and quite a bit less expensive than "justice," the notion of "opportunity" is a principle so pure, so abstract, and so empty that nobody will be safe from its dictates. It is invariably used as a pure positive, as if opportunity came about through the alchemy of generosity and creativity, something that blossoms as soon as the obstacles to it are removed. A moment's reflection shows that it is precisely through the notion of opportunity that the world looks "available," ripe for the picking. Although it might originally have seemed like a relatively innocent economic term, where it signals a lack of regulation or constraint, it now seems plausible that wars of all kinds will be fought in the name of "opportunity," whatever it may turn out to mean.

Throughout both texts, every globalist or universalist high note is answered by the solid thump of patriotic affirmation. This duality becomes a constant refrain. The 2002 NSS calls for "a distinctly American internationalism," based on the certainty that the US represents the "single sustainable model for national success: freedom, democracy, and free enterprise." The 2010 NSS does not use the same words, but pushes the same message in its concluding celebration of "our founding documents" and "the creed that binds us together" as the very source of truth that will "renew American leadership in the world." The signature contradiction is right there: all people share our ideals, but nobody can match us and nobody can judge us. This contradiction becomes especially acute in the face of the epochal changes evoked by both documents: on one hand, the US wants to move toward the new paradigm of the fully networked "market-state," but it somehow wishes that it could be the only one capable of using such power. Ideally, the US would stand somewhere above the fray of the market itself: always first among unequals. What appears here as a conceptual glitch or uncensored dream may actually signal the pivotal predicament of the last superpower, henceforth uncertain whether its military superiority will guarantee its lucrative position as the guardian of world markets. For the rest of the world, this uncertainty means wondering how much longer the supremacy of the US will seem desirable, convincing, or necessary.

As soon as we begin to doubt that this contradiction can be resolved with a few rhetorical turns, both versions of the NSS begin to look less like concise statements of principles and more like mixed bags of maneuvers: mouthing empty support here, asserting an iron will there, crafting evasive euphemisms in one paragraph and insinuating serious threats in the next. In such circumstances, the line between advertising American virtue and issuing imperial commands becomes rather blurry. In the end these texts serve a simple ideological function: they render superfluous any criticism of US policy based on charges of hypocrisy, inconsistency, unfairness, or ruthlessness. Those kinds of criticism, which belong to a public sphere premised on dialogue and accountability, are here preempted by millennial phrases about global supremacy, universal values, and the prerogatives of power. In their book *Multitude*, Michael Hardt and Antonio Negri argue that "violence is legitimated most effectively today . . . not on any a priori framework, moral or legal, but only a posteriori, based on its results."[22] That sounds right as far as it goes, but it is necessary to take the next step and say that therefore the whole question of the legitimation of violence belongs to the imaginary realm of media strategies, rather than the symbolic realm of political and legal institutions.

In their internal inconsistencies and flagrant insincerities, both documents actually register the ghostly traces of what stands against them. But the drama of negotiation, or even the possibility of opposition, is never acknowledged. The grain of truth of each NSS consists in the way it withdraws into its own kind of wishful thinking and dreamy phrasing in the face of every real gap between "the world as it is" and "the world we seek," refusing to make any binding

22   Michael Hardt and Antonio Negri, *Multitude* (New York: Penguin Press, 2004), p. 30.

promises and reserving the right to decide every issue that might otherwise be invoked to contest its authority. Indeed, by packaging its authority this way, the American state effectively suspends it, withdrawing it from political and legal contestation. The highest form of sovereignty, it turns out, is the ability to live entirely within one's pretenses, resorting to brute force whenever necessary to make reality conform.

The rest of us cannot afford to see things from those commanding heights, and even when invited to do so by the evening news or the op-ed pages, we should firmly refuse. Faced with the strategic mobilization of the public sphere, we are on the way to discovering just how little consent it takes to keep the whole apparatus running. The prospect of unending warfare should seem no more like inevitable destiny than the vision of free markets should seem like divinely ordained providence. The world-picture of the market-state, organized by the ever more intimate fusion of war and trade, is finally believable only from the perspective of the generals, central bankers, and TV pundits. Its "freedoms" belong most securely to the very rich, their enforcers, and their mouthpieces. For everybody else caught up in this historical moment, endless war is still a matter of working under daily threat, carrying out labors with no triumphal purpose, each day ending with either "annihilation or a lucky break" as the case may be.[23] In uncertain days like these, when lucky breaks seem harder and harder to count on, nobody needs to lend a hand or a heart or a mind to those who threaten annihilation and call it peace.

Under the present circumstances, it is hard to know where to turn. The current regime of indebtedness is designed to make everyone (or almost everyone) pay now for a system of violence that may yet turn against them. How is it possible to reverse, or deflect, or evade this assault? Let me end with a story, or rather two stories, taken from a multipart text titled "Air Raid on Halberstadt, April 8, 1945," by

23   Oskar Negt and Alexander Kluge, *Geschichte und Eigensinn*, Band II *Der unterschätzte Mensch* (Frankfurt am Main: Zweitausendeins, 2002), p. 820.

the great German writer, filmmaker, and theorist Alexander Kluge.[24] These two stories are juxtaposed in the midst of many others, all concerned with human behavior during a very specific, very deadly moment. The first piece, titled "Strategy from Below," describes the actions and thoughts of a schoolteacher, Gerda Baethe, who finds herself in a cellar with her three children as the bombs start falling. What can she do? She looks around, tries to guess how close the explosions are, whether they are coming her way; she appraises the sturdiness of the houses nearby, judges how quickly she can get the children to run across the yard. But all of this will not be enough—it is merely a tactical evasion of an enemy she cannot see or predict. Instead, she tries to think strategically, to imagine the whole town, to predict where the fires have already blocked the escape routes. She tries to outsmart the bombers. But, Kluge notes, it is too late. Her only chance to develop an effective strategy against the bombers did not occur that morning or even the night before, or in 1939, or in 1933 . . . but in 1918, at the end of the previous war, when she would have had to join with thousands of other teachers, to organize and teach "hard," in order to build lasting social relationships that might have blocked the rise of the Nazis. But Gerda learns the lesson of November 1918 in April 1945: *Once upon a time, it would have been possible to turn history around.*

The next story is titled "Strategy from Above." It documents the other side of the situation: after all, the bombers did not come from nowhere. There had to have been long-term industrial planning, intensive technical research, and extensive cooperative labor relationships so that these massive and deadly objects could now move at tremendous speed in the sky above, efficient instruments of a strategic plan developed hundreds of miles away. Kluge provides a full dossier: charts of the different kinds of bombs (titled "the goods"), photographs, reports from legal authorities, and diagrams

---

24   Alexander Kluge, *Chronik der Gefühle*, Band II (Suhrkamp, 2004), pp. 43–66.

of plane formations, all supplemented with an interview conducted years later between a German reporter and the American bombardier. The reporter wants to learn about the procedures of an air raid: What did you have for breakfast, how were the orders given, how did the people in the cockpit understand their tasks? The American is perfectly frank: they had a job to do and they did it. It was routine, they didn't even have to look out of the window. The reporter is curious: Was there any way you would have broken off the attack? Could the people of the city have done anything to stop the attack? Flying a white flag? No, no, no. The primary targets, the secondary targets, and the targets of opportunity were already laid out by bomber command in England. The bombs had to be dropped before the planes could return to base—it was only a question of where and when.

Without a doubt, the teacher in the cellar exemplifies one of the characteristic experiences of modernity. On 9/11, some people in the United States were surprised to learn that it was still possible to feel that way. For a few hours, the hijackers monopolized the standpoint above; only later, after they were dead, was it seized back by the US military and the TV networks. But citizens of the major powers need not feel stuck in the standpoint below for very long. The media's world-picture is designed to offer all the visceral thrills and psychic compensations that accompany the standpoint above. We are granted such a privilege precisely insofar as we have no practical way of acting on it. If we accept these arrangements, we never have to feel locked up in the imaginary cellars for very long; the feeling of being threatened quickly gives way to renewed calls to arms, and spectators can once again feel the buzz of the war room. The fastest short-circuit leaps from abject fear to bloody ruthlessness. After 9/11, this shift took about two days, as the networks moved from passive displays of patriotism to firm calls for revenge and an attitude of relentlessly aggressive readiness. The war in Afghanistan, now under new management, is still running on that buzz.

So when the talk shows convene panels of pundits to debate the ongoing war on terror, the only real differences of opinion concern when and where to drop the bombs. These convivial gabfests, peppered by frequent commercial breaks, would seem like merely irrelevant chatter if we didn't keep in mind that it is precisely this sort of chatter that will indeed guide the bombs onward to their next destination. (A random example plucked from the airwaves in January 2009: Fareed Zakaria asks the Afghan foreign minister on CNN: "Are we killing the wrong people right now?" In what kind of conversation would that be an acceptable question? Merely listening to such glib cruelty feels like a war crime.)

It is exactly the same with the economic crisis: the standpoint above has been adapted for use by market wizards and gnomic bankers, who pronounce upon the chances of prosperity and poverty for the world's billions. Every so-called debate, whether it concerns the wisdom of structural adjustment or the morality of aid, revolves around the need to maintain imperial power and its dignity, and to preserve economic supremacy and its perks. Without exception the major media have proven to be completely committed to this kind of expert strategic thinking: they will supply the news and the range of acceptable opinions to go along with it as long as we can be trusted to treat it "from above," inviting us to be co-conspirators as soon as we turn on the TV. The daily media feed is framed by the imperative that strategic thinking should orient everybody's action and rhetoric: no matter how distant or powerless you might feel, you can now take part in the standpoint above, armed with orbiting media networks, state-of-the-art firepower, and all the trading tools you need to commit yourself to the wheel of fortune. The public sphere has been programmed for an unending war, which will prove to be nothing other than the perpetual peace of globalized markets.

We'd better hope, urgently and passionately and against all appearances, that we can still learn from the schoolteacher in Kluge's story. We certainly do not want to imagine ourselves stuck there in the cellar, already under attack by forces we can no longer grasp. And so it would be better to restart the lesson at an earlier moment, when the teacher is just beginning to wonder what's happening around her and asking what she can do about it, when she is still capable of organizing to block the catastrophes already being prepared, long before the bombers have appeared—when she can still imagine that the story is not already over.

Bono and Bush at the White House, March 14, 2002 © AP Photo/Ron Edmonds

4   Letter to Bono

You ought to know that this letter isn't really addressed to you. I want to make an argument about the role of spectacle in the politics of global poverty, and I imagine that you are the person least likely to be convinced by what I have to say. So this letter is addressed not to you, not to a person, but to him, the persona, the media image known as Bono. That grandiose and ubiquitous image has become the public face of global poverty, and that is precisely the problem.

This letter takes its cue from a 1972 film by Jean-Luc Godard and Jean-Pierre Gorin titled *Letter to Jane*. Their film is a cinematic letter, composed in images and sounds, addressed to Jane Fonda. Shortly after making a movie with them titled *Tout va bien*, Fonda had gone to North Vietnam, where she conducted a highly publicized tour of bombed villages. Godard and Gorin sent their cinematic letter as a response to the press coverage of Fonda's trip to Vietnam. For most of the film we see just one image, a magazine photograph of Fonda in Vietnam. We hear Godard and Gorin talking about the image at great length, examining its details and questioning its possible uses. They want to investigate the way Fonda put her celebrity to use on behalf of the North Vietnamese, who were under ferocious assault by the US military. Although Godard and Gorin admire her impulse to help the Vietnamese people, they say that her gesture of solidarity is insufficient and contradictory. After thoroughly criticizing her stance and her actions, they invite her to reply. As far as I know, she never answered their letter, either in words or in images. In recent years she has, however, apologized profusely for being "thoughtless" about the publicity generated by her trip. As someone who knows the power of images, Fonda has said, she should have known better.

Even when set against such a doubtful precedent, celebrity politics has clearly regressed. In 1972, Jane Fonda went to see for herself what happens when B-52s drop their bombs on villages and towns. In 1985, a crowd of rock stars (organized by Bob Geldof and including Bono) staged two huge concerts called Live Aid to raise money for starving people in Ethiopia. The money helped to buy supplies in an emergency, although press reports have shown that the effort was deflected by local conflicts and even by superpower maneuvering around the Horn of Africa. In 2005, another crowd of rock stars (led by Geldof and Bono) performed at a series of concerts called Live8. Here the goal was meant to be unambiguous: the event would support and publicize the development agenda proposed at the summit of G8 leaders in Gleneagles, Scotland. At each turn of this history, the call for political commitment becomes less and less critical, less and less tangible, less and less committed. The logic of this evolution—during which every trace of opposition, intransigence, and negativity disappears—leads to a well-behaved "activism" that becomes little more than the pop-cultural expression of official policy.

Bono surely knows that the economic and ideological machinery that creates global rock superstars is inseparable from the vast machinery that creates and maintains global poverty. He says that he wants to be seen as a tough businessman playing by pragmatic rules rather than a do-gooder invoking his exalted ideals. He refuses no accolade, no medal, no knighthood; it does not appear to have occurred to him that the praise and honors heaped on him by pundits and politicians might belong to the repertoire of empty gestures whereby the custodians of the system grandly congratulate themselves for having some kind of a conscience. Within that system Bono has been quite successful: he has gained extraordinary access to presidents, ministers, and corporate leaders; he attends summit meetings and private audiences; and he has assembled a network of supporters to provide expertise and publicity. He believes that his superstar presence can move world leaders to address global poverty, and he casts his campaign as a rebellion and a crusade. But the more often he succeeds within this system, the more clear it becomes that his political agenda is really theirs, and that his way of doing politics does an injustice to everybody he claims to represent. By joining in the merry-go-round of promises, deferrals, disappointments, and compromises—that whole sorry spectacle—Bono is doing his part, more than his part, to prevent real change to the global system that causes poverty.

Instead of arguing about policy, strategy, and morality—we can leave that to the policy makers, strategists, and moralists—let's examine precisely *what Bono does*. First of all, in order to operate in the arena of politics, he has had to leverage his show biz fame into the currency of official connections and news media attention. "Bono," the rock star persona, has become a kind of living brand name capable of functioning in a wide variety of settings. Strictly speaking, the power of this public image doesn't belong to one person, and it has little to do with personal qualities like charm or talent. The image of "Bono" is actually a very big production, carefully constructed by many people over a long time, crafted to fulfill a range of practical purposes, from selling CDs and iPods to fundraising, sponsoring, and lobbying. Meanwhile the flesh-and-blood Bono has to be an expert at multiplying, amplifying, inflecting, and enacting images of himself; that is the special skill and expertise he has to offer, the unique source of his authority. Not everyone could pull it off. He has to strike a tricky balance between making himself visible and making himself scarce, massively larger than life and intimately down-to-earth. His role is to inhabit that image in just the right way, stoking its aura of popularity—its market value—in order to attach it to actual products, tasks, and agendas.

Take a look at the photograph of Bono and George W. Bush. It was taken by the AP photographer Ron Edmonds on March 14, 2002, and quickly disseminated around the world, via newspapers, magazines, and the Internet. According to the caption, Bono and President George W. Bush are walking across the White House lawn after a meeting at the Inter-American Development Bank. What does this image tell us?

First of all, there are two gestures and two looks. Bono is holding up his right hand, giving a V-sign. It is not immediately obvious what that gesture means here, especially because he is not at all the only person to have shown it on the White House lawn. Does it mean victory over the Vietnamese, like Nixon? Victory over the Soviets, like Reagan? Or is it supposed to be a peace sign? If so, peace for whom, exactly? Is he perhaps signaling a victory for peace, or peace with victory, or something else entirely? Meanwhile, Bush is holding up his right hand with the palm up. It could be a friendly wave but it could also be an imperious salute. This ambivalent gesture is also common on the White House lawn, where greeting friends and giving orders usually amounts to the same thing. Bono is looking directly at the camera. His mouth is closed and his whole face is composed and ready for display. Bush, on the other hand, is slightly turned away, glancing somewhere else, and his mouth is open as if he were trying to smile. Bono seems to have decided that he cannot afford to smile. His expression is tight and serious; Bush's is perfunctory and distracted. Their clothes tell the opposite story: Bush's suit is buttoned up and he's wearing a tie; Bono's jacket is open, showing an open shirt, untucked. Bono looks slouchy and rumpled, pausing for the camera, while Bush keeps walking ahead, scarcely lingering or turning. Bono looks determined, even heroic, in a well-practiced way, while Bush looks stiff, distant, and unconcerned.

The photograph is a calculated risk for both of them. An image like this is a deliberate act, a public statement, perhaps even a kind of promise. Insofar as the two of them have different agendas at stake—a supposition we will examine in a minute—it should be obvious that the existence and dissemination of this photograph will serve those agendas differently and unequally. What serves one of them in the short term may serve the other in the long run, and it is hard to say which of them is playing the longer game. So although both of them are equally visible in the photograph, they are not really there in the same way.

To a well-trained, cynical viewer, this photo does not need to be decoded at all, because the cynicism is built right into it. The image does not simply advertise that some kind of deal is being struck: the image is the substance of the deal itself.[1] The only question is whether or not it is a good deal, and for whom.

It is easy to imagine what people will say: Bono and Bush are simply using each other. Bono uses his celebrity to pressure Bush on debt relief and AIDS funding for Africa. Bush uses Bono to show that he is somehow in touch with popular tastes, and somehow sympathetic to the causes Bono espouses. Nobody will be surprised to see the pomp of state power mingling so freely with the glitz of pop stardom. Nobody needs to believe that these two men are actually having a serious conversation about the issues of global poverty. Instead everybody will assume that each of them has a good, if vague, reason to be seen in public with the other. For Bono, this photo might provide a kind of blackmail, to be used at some later date to

---

1   In a cover story on Bono for the *New York Times Sunday Magazine,* James Traub reports that this initial photo opportunity was brokered by Condoleezza Rice. In exchange for his presence beside Bush, Bono originally demanded that Bush would announce a new AIDS funding initiative. On the day before the event, he learned that there would be no such announcement, but Bono went along anyway, hoping to convince Bush later. As we will see, it is a pattern that would be repeated throughout the following years. (James Traub, "The Statesman," *New York Times Sunday Magazine*, September 18, 2005, pp. 87–9.) Contrast this glowing press coverage with attacks from the left (George Monbiot, "Bards of the Powerful," *Guardian*, June 21, 2005; available online: monbiot.com) and the free-trade faithful (Jagdish Bhagwati, "A noble effort to end poverty, Bono, but it is misdirected," *Financial Times*, February 28, 2006, p. 13).

remind the president to keep his promises. For Bush, it might be an alibi, offered up whenever someone complains about his insensitivity to poverty. Bono supporters can see it as a breakthrough in the campaign to wangle a commitment from the administration, while Bush supporters can see it as proof that the president's conservatism really is compassionate after all. Yet the reverse reading seems equally plausible: Bono is not there to push his own agenda, but to support Bush's, and in exchange Bush will help Bono gain access to *his* constituency, legislators, policy makers, "world leaders," lobbyists, and various rich people.

Bono might think that he got the better end of the bargain. All he had to do was to let himself be paraded before the cameras; Bush was the one who was supposed to commit political capital and real money. The only thing Bono had to give up was imaginary capital, a momentary scrap of his public persona, and he has plenty of that to offer. But the deal cuts both ways. Just as Bono surrenders the rebellious image of a rock-and-roll singer, Bush demonstrates how even the most unanswerable and withdrawn forms of state power rely on the ceaseless conjuring of spectacle.

Let's look more closely at this event from 2002. What role is Bono playing in this negotiation? When campaigning for debt relief, whose side is he on? Does he take the side of the creditors, eager to get their money back? Does he take the side of the highly indebted governments, anxious to improve their position in the world market? Or does he somehow speak on behalf of indebted people in general, who are desperate to get out from under an economic structure that crushes the life out of them?

Let's not forget that the "debt relief" bill passed by Congress in 2000, which marked Bono's first foray into US political lobbying, did not directly appropriate new money to aid the poor. Instead, the $435 million appropriation was a kind of internal bookkeeping measure to erase existing bilateral debt owed to the US government. (This was simply the stub end of the original debts, which had been discounted over the years already.) The debt relief measure, passed in a year when the US was running a large budget surplus, seemed neither courageous nor particularly generous. Remember that "debt relief" amounts to paying off creditors holding onerous, possibly unpayable, debts. As long as they get a good share of what they're owed, the creditors love it. Bankers and bondholders see a payday they thought might never come. Governments who write off debt can use the occasion to place new conditions on future lending and aid. As for the ostensibly humanitarian benefits of debt relief, everything depends on the political situation of the indebted countries. Although the financial balance sheets of poor nations certainly improve when debt service obligations are reduced, there may be little real impact on the quality of life for poor people.

That is why the issue of debt relief necessarily raises historical and political questions about the way such debts have been contracted, enforced, and unequally imposed across whole societies and the whole world. There is, to say the least, always a disparity between the official parties who contract debts and the multitude of people who try to live under the burdens of sovereign indebtedness. In the contemporary global economy, indebtedness should not be viewed as the accidental product of bad luck or poor planning: as we have seen, it functions everywhere as a regime of top-down control and network discipline, designed to replace older forms of social negotiation and political autonomy. As this regime becomes entrenched, every dimension of social life will be restructured according to the wishes of the creditors and their local enforcers, rationing access to everything from work and education to clean water and air, subjecting every component of the local economy to increasingly direct pressures from the global markets. Throughout the global south, this process has been going on for decades; indeed, depending on the way we connect the dots between enslavement, colonization, and indebtedness, it has

been going on for centuries. And that is why the full cancellation of debts should, in principle, empower a genuine liberation
of indebted people, not only from financial obligations imposed
upon them by foreign and domestic creditors, but from political
domination by their own ruling elites. And yet it never seems to
work out that way—why?

We should return to Bush's speech at the Inter-American Bank,
which marked a renewed effort to link US aid to neoliberal policy
prescriptions for the developing world. In the March 2002 speech
Bush announced the Millennium Challenge Account, his administration's response to the United Nations' Millennium Development
Goals, the UN's signature initiative to address the life-and-death
crisis in the developing world. Bush insisted that aid must involve
"accountability" for both rich and poor governments, signaling that
the existing "conditionality" clauses were still too weak and that
future aid would be more closely supervised and more narrowly
targeted than before. And to prove that this program served the
highest of purposes, he linked the effort to help developing nations
to the global war on terror. When it came to specifics, he offered a
$5 billion annual increase, built up over the next three years. This
budget figure must have caught Bono's attention right away. The
UN Millennium Goals, crafted in 2000 under the supervision of his
mentor, Jeffrey Sachs, called for substantial increases in foreign aid
and major improvements in the human welfare of poor nations. So
it would have been immediately obvious that the Bush Millennium
Challenge fell far short of the commitments the United States had
already made. As Sachs himself has pointed out, Bush's pledge of $5
billion, even if fulfilled, would have been less than 0.05 percent of a
single year's GNP, whereas the UN goals (agreed upon by the UN
members themselves) called for rich countries to give 0.7 percent
a year by 2015. Indeed, Sachs excoriated Bush's 2002 speech for the
"disconnect" between its analysis of the problems facing poor countries (with which he was nevertheless in fundamental agreement)

and the paltry sums it offered as a solution.[2] We can assume that Bono realized that Bush was massively undercutting the Millennium Goals, but he showed no sign of it, sitting there on stage or, later, walking across the White House lawn for the photographers.

Today it is clear that the Millennium Challenge initiative has accomplished very little beyond diminishing expectations about the commitment of the US government to helping the world's poor. Let's follow the time line laid out by Bush in 2002, projecting four years into the future. First, it took more than two years to set up the initiative's new bureaucracy, the Millennium Challenge Corporation. The MCC has never been anywhere close to fully funded; instead of $10 billion over three years, Congress appropriated only $4.25 billion. Out of that, the MCC actually approved only $1.6 billion worth of projects, and of that sum, it managed to disburse only about $19.5 million.[3] Look at those numbers again: out of the already inadequate sums promised on that day in March 2002, after four years less than one-fifth had even been earmarked for particular countries, and of that, just a tiny fraction (less than 2 percent of the total) had actually been sent anywhere. But the chronic underfunding and inefficiency of the MCC goes hand in hand with its repudiation of state-led development and its starve-the-beast attitude toward official aid. Its programs have little to do with the commonsense life-saving items Bono likes to emphasize in his sales pitch (malaria bed nets and village wells): the money is largely aimed at infrastructure (ports and roads) and at developing private sector businesses in agriculture, tourism, and finance. Indeed, the MCC ranks prospective recipients

---

2   Jeffrey Sachs, *The End of Poverty: Economic Possibilities for Our Time* (New York: Penguin Press, 2005), p. 337.

3   Michael A. Fletcher and Paul Blustein, "With New Leader, Foreign Aid Program Is Taking Off," *Washington Post*, January 31, 2006, p. A15. Also see Celia W. Dugger, "U.S. Agency's Slow Pace Endangers Foreign Aid," *New York Times*, December 7, 2007, p. 1. Dugger reports that the disbursements by the end of 2007 had only reached $155 million, out of $4.8 billion approved. Current data on disbursements and contracts is available online at mcc.gov.

using an array of indicators produced by the Heritage Foundation, Freedom House, the World Bank, and others. That's the deal that Bono has been promoting ever since: an urgent call to save lives turns out to be a protracted campaign to spread free enterprise.

By way of contrast, consider the money spent on the Iraq war and reconstruction over the same period, through January 2006: $251 billion. During the same period that the administration had such a hard time scraping together just over $4 billion for the Millennium Challenge, it spent more than *sixty times* that much on Iraq. As *Financial Times* columnist Martin Wolf noted, "the minimum budgetary cost [of the war] is 10 times the world's net annual official development assistance to all developing countries."[4] (Congressional appropriations for the Iraq War would reach $748 billion by the spring of 2010, plus another $53 billion for reconstruction.[5]) Moreover, there are costs not counted by the budget, including health care for veterans and the cost in American lives. In 2008, Joseph Stiglitz and Linda Bilmes estimated that the total economic costs of the war (not counting the cost in Iraqi lives) would likely rise to as much as $3 trillion.[6] If the US government can spend so much money when it wants badly to do something and does not care how much it costs, we can begin to calculate how little it cares about Africa. (Of course the same lesson can be drawn from the financial crisis: billions for bailing out banks, insurance companies, and hedge funds, while scarcely a trickle of money goes to support those most at risk from a global downturn.)

Bait-and-switch maneuvers also prevailed in Bush's AIDS policy in Africa. The dollars and percentages announced with great fanfare did not materialize, and even the substantial funds that were spent

---

4   Martin Wolf, "America failed to calculate the enormous costs of war," *Financial Times*, January 11, 2006. Available online: ft.com.

5   Matthew Duss, Peter Juul, and Brian Katulis, "The Iraq War Ledger," released May 6, 2010, online at americanprogress.org.

6   Joseph Stiglitz and Linda Bilmes, *The Three Trillion Dollar War: The True Cost of the Iraq Conflict* (New York: W.W. Norton, 2008).

have been channeled into a strikingly contentious agenda. The administration's strategy was marked on one side by its legal and financial support of big pharmaceutical corporations hoping to squelch poor countries' manufacture of generic drugs, and on the other side by its heavy emphasis on abstinence and monogamy as the keys to prevention. More people did indeed receive anti-retroviral drugs than before, because the US government brokered a patent-protection deal with the Big Pharma companies. Surely this strategy has its costs. Should we count the number of people "saved" by the pro-patent approach against the number of people who might have been saved if the patents had simply been broken by the endangered countries? And who can quantify the damage done by narrowly moralizing public health campaigns? As long as the standard of performance begins with "better than nothing," there will always be a semblance of progress even if nothing really changes. But it is difficult to celebrate the number of people "alive today" because of President Bush's policies—which is Bono's constant refrain—without asking whether more people might be alive if different priorities had prevailed. Or to put it another way: whenever a superpower trumpets the lives it has saved in one place, it is absolutely necessary to ask about the lives it has taken elsewhere.

Even when the carrots don't materialize, the stick always does. Bush's hard-nosed rhetoric of "accountability" has become a keynote in discussions about foreign aid. What that means in practice can be judged by the way successive administrations claimed to be spreading "freedom" around the world under the banner of the Washington Consensus: those countries rendered pliable and docile will be hailed as truly democratic, while those that balk at following orders from Washington will be treated as outcasts. It is not a question of whether aid should require "enforced liberalization": that issue has already been settled, by force. Where the rigors of liberalization and the surrender of sovereign priorities have already taken place, aid and investment will flow more freely, and where it has not, aid will be parceled out for smaller and narrower purposes. Any challenges to this regimen—as when the democratically elected government of Bolivia considers nationalizing the gas industry—are met with stern warnings and open threats. "Accountability" is the next turn of the screw beyond "conditionality": it means more strict scrutiny by the donors and more inbred obedience for the recipients. This approach reaps the rewards of IMF austerity plans, even as it acknowledges their failures. We can expect that debt relief will be granted only in those places where decades of debt peonage have already had their usual effects: a thoroughly stripped and restructured economy, a weakened state, and an eviscerated civil society. On such blighted earth, new kinds of dependency, rebranded as "freedoms," will surely grow.

Back in 2002, Bush reiterated his plans for "developing nations" at the Monterrey Conference and, more significantly, in his National Security Strategy document, released in September 2002. That document, as we have seen, calls for US economic and military domination of the world, enshrines free trade as a "moral principle," and justifies the use of preemptive force against any threat. Over the years Bono has had plenty of time to think about how all of this fits together. Has there been any reason to assume, then or now, that he has ever really disagreed with any part of the administration's global strategy? From one photo opportunity to the next, the images of Bono and Bush kept telling the same stories—the major new policy announcements, the public haggling over percentages, the congratulations on unprecedented achievements, the request for more money next time. Just as the dire evocations of an "emergency" never let up, neither does the humble and optimistic plea to try harder. In order to embrace these contradictions, we are supposed to get used to the disjuncture between visionary plans, disappointing follow-through, and ongoing catastrophe. We are asked to brace ourselves for the long haul, always keeping up the pressure, subscribing to the every-little-bit-helps approach to big problems. In this way, we grow accustomed to the impression that there is only one way to address global poverty (let's call it messianic neoliberalism), that its basic principles are indisputable and widely shared, and that the only real discussion is taking place between Bono and various heads of state. We are meant to accept that such conversations (always commemorated with another photo op) exhaust the spectrum of possibilities for the world's poor. And yet, looking at political developments across the global south, it is easy to see that Bono's unending charm offensive is not the only hope; in fact, it is not the best hope—it is not much of a hope at all.

Over the course of 2005, Bono's image took on a new ubiquity, especially during the media blitz surrounding Live8 and the Gleneagles G8 meeting. As Jamie Drummond wrote, "Live8 and the G8 Summit garnered this year more than 2.7 billion media impressions in America alone according to our best estimates."[7] It is striking that Drummond speaks as if Live8 and the G8 meeting were the same event. It is hard to know what a "media impression" is—let alone what kind of significance 2.7 billion of them might have—but let us take note of one televisual event: Bono's appearance on *Meet the Press* on June 26. Bono's face and voice were being transmitted from Dublin to the studio in Washington, so that Tim Russert could interview him "live." Just moments before, Russert had interviewed Donald Rumsfeld about the war in Iraq.

Even though Bono wasn't in the same studio as Rumsfeld, he shared the same program, separated only by a few commercials for financial services companies, Boeing Aerospace, and the agricultural conglomerate Archer Daniels Midland. It's easy to see that all of these images fit together nicely. From moment to moment, television has an ineluctable way of making connections, sometimes surprising and sometimes not surprising at all.

---

7   Jamie Drummond, DATA website. Posted at data.org/archives; accessed January 12, 2006. The DATA group (Debt Aid Trade Africa) merged with Bono's ONE group in 2007.

Russert asked Bono a number of good questions. Concerning Live8, he asked if it was true that Bono and Geldof had agreed to steer clear of any critique of Bush and Blair over the Iraq war. Bono replied, "Absolutely. This is the other war. This is a war that can be won so much more easily than the war against terror, and we wish the president and others luck in winning the war against terror." Concerning the "accountability" of aid for Africa, he told Russert:

This is the number-one problem facing Africa: corruption. Not natural calamity, not the AIDS virus. This is the number-one issue and there's no way around it. That's what was so clever about President Bush's Millennium Challenge. It was start-up money for new democracies. It was giving increases of aid flows only to countries that are tackling corruption. That's what's so clever. It's—the implementation of the Millennium Challenge has not happened. It is in trouble. They recognize that. President Bush is embarrassed about that. They're trying to put it right. But the idea, the concept, was a great one.[8]

We've already seen just how narrowly focused and badly funded the Millennium Challenge Corporation was. Nevertheless Bono offered his full support once again, performing damage control for the Bush Administration at a crucial moment. No wonder the State Department posted a proud news release the day after this broadcast, headlined "US Aid to Africa Hits Record Levels; Geldof, Bono praise Bush before Group of Eight Summit in Scotland."[9]

---

8   NBC News, *Meet the Press*, transcript for June 26, 2005, p. 23. Available online: msnbc.msn.com.

9   State Department, "Rock Star Bono Applauds Bush Efforts to Aid Africa, Cites AIDS Funding, Anti-corruption Element of Millennium Challenge Account," news release created June 27, revised June 28, 2005. Available online: america.gov. It is worth noting that the State Department webmasters used the Associated Press photo of Bush and Bono from March 2002 to illustrate their story.

Just a few minutes earlier on the broadcast, Russert had asked Donald Rumsfeld about the progress of the war on terror and the prospects for democracy in Iraq. Rumsfeld replied:

> [The] Iraqi people have a choice. They're either going to go down a dark path where the beheadings are, and a small group of people who run that whole country, as they have before, or they're going to have a representative system, where women participate and where people have to have protections against each other because of the constitution. And I think they're going to choose a path of lightness. There's—the sweep of human history is for freedom. Look at what's happened in Lebanon and Kurdistan and the Ukraine and these countries. I think there's—we can be optimistic about the future, but we have to recognize that it's a tough, tough, tough world, and there are going to be a lot of bumps in the road between now and then.[10]

Is the Defense Secretary's visionary optimism, tempered with hardheaded realism, really all that different from Bono's? One is fighting poverty and corruption in Africa; the other is fighting an insurgency in Iraq. We keep hearing that it is the same war, without metaphor, as far as the eye can see.

While interviewing Bono, Russert replayed a portion of the ONE campaign ad, which includes this statement by Nelson Mandela: "We now need leadership, precision, and political courage." Russert remarked, "'Political courage.' Those words seem to be a direct challenge to President Bush and the other leaders." To which Bono responded: "Yeah. Yeah, it is a challenge." He praised European countries for boosting their development aid (as a percentage of GDP), while "the United States is down to about .17 [percent]; .2 is within sight. But really to get serious about this, the United States has to get up to .3, .4, .5. That's our wish here. And we know it will take time to

---

10   *Meet the Press* transcript, p. 4.

get there. We know that you've got a deficit problem. We understand there's a war being fought."[11]

Underline these numbers. Bono casually suggests that the US might raise the level of aid to 0.3, 0.4, or 0.5 percent of GDP. He must know that such an increase would require multiplying that Millennium Challenge promise three, five, or seven times. And given the difference between promises, specific agreements, and actual disbursements, it is clear that the whole aid system would have to grow more efficient and effective by several orders of magnitude in order to deliver the money. Given everything—that president, that Congress, that deficit, that war—this was simply not a serious wish. Russert did not raise a challenge, and viewers could hardly decide if Bono was admirably stubborn about his demands or simply disingenuous. To speak of such goals without speaking of the need to make fundamental changes in the political situation is not dreamy idealism, it's disinformation. In the mass media division of labor, politicians lie about facts and celebrities lie about hopes.

We can also set aside the question of whether or not this increase in aid would really do so much good, whether it would solve the problems of developing countries or "make poverty history." We need not enter into the arguments about how aid might be spent, although that is clearly a crucial issue. (The economist Robert Pollin has made a reasonable argument that Bono's proposal for aid in alliance with a neoliberal trade regime will be strikingly worse than an effort to build an alternative to neoliberalism.[12]) For our purposes

---

11   *Ibid.*, p. 21.

12   Robert Pollin, *Contours of Descent: US Economic Fractures and the Landscape of Global Austerity* (London: Verso, 2003), pp. 163–8. Meanwhile, questions about the effectiveness of aid in the execution of contemporary imperial rule have been raised by the former World Bank economist William Easterly, in *The White Man's Burden* (New York: Penguin Books, 2006), and the former Goldman Sachs economist Dambisa Moyo, in *Dead Aid* (New York: Farrar, Straus & Giroux, 2009). Moyo enjoyed a brief season of positive press coverage as the "anti-Bono" for her calls to end all development aid and to impose shock therapy prescriptions on African governments. When Sachs protested against such a plan, she gleefully pointed out that she had learned the recipe from him when she was a student at Harvard.

here, on the level of images, it is enough to show just how much euphemism and misdirection have to be employed in order to make Bono's campaign look disinterested and philanthropic, even as it allies itself with the most aggressive imperial powers.

Earlier in the broadcast, Russert quoted a statement by Rumsfeld's former deputy, Paul Wolfowitz, who testified to Congress in March 2003, "We're dealing with a country [Iraq] that can really finance its reconstruction relatively soon . . . [The] oil revenues of that country could bring in between $50 and $100 billion over the course of the next two or three years." Russert then asked Rumsfeld, "Did you make a misjudgment about the cost of the war?" And Rumsfeld dismissed the question with a shrug: "I never estimated the cost of the war. And how can one estimate the cost in lives or the cost in money? I've avoided it consistently."[13] In his years directing the war, Rumsfeld had his own way with numbers, which was also his way with human lives: he didn't consider them at all.

When Wolfowitz was catastrophically wrong about the costs of the Iraq war, he was rewarded for his expertise with the presidency of the World Bank, a tenure that proved to be short-lived. He made a show of wanting to talk with Bono soon after his installation there, and Bono promptly took his calls. Later Wolfowitz met with Bono backstage at Live8, as the World Bank proudly advertised on its web pages. Rumsfeld, Condoleezza Rice, Robert Gates, and the rest of the administration remained openly dismissive of any attempt to count human costs along the "path of lightness." How could Bono put himself in such company and still invoke the moral authority of Nelson Mandela? Remember Mandela's criticisms of the rush to war: "[The] attitude of the United States of America is a threat to world peace . . . [There] is no doubt that the United States now feels that they are the only superpower in the world and they can do what they like."[14] Throughout the Bush administration, no matter what

---

13   *Meet the Press* transcript, p. 13.
14   Nelson Mandela, interview, "The United States Is a Threat to World Peace," *Newsweek*, September 10, 2002.

happened, Bono continued to do business with the president as well as with those around him. The images remained the same, even as the agendas changed: a smile and a handshake, again and again.

By the end of 2005, mainstream media commentary was cautiously optimistic about the debt relief, aid, and trade agreements hammered out in the wake of the G8 meeting. There was widespread recognition that these deals were not all that they had first appeared to be, let alone all that was needed. Once again, well-trained cynics denounced the extravagant hype surrounding the whole event, and keen-eyed critics noticed that the deals were whittled down in the process of implementation. As before, the distinction between the erasure of old debts and the provision of new aid was absolutely crucial, yet was left notably blurry in the official pronouncements. Nevertheless, it might seem especially churlish to deny that something good happened, and that the Make Poverty History (MPH) campaign played a significant role in shaping that outcome.

In order to accept that version of the story, however, we would have to believe that Bono, Geldof, and the MPH campaign effectively marshaled "public opinion" into a collective body capable of pressuring the G8 governments and the multilateral financial institutions. We would have to believe that all of those so-called "media impressions," along with a year-long blitz of white wristbands, public rallies, mass concerts, TV commercials, Internet petitions, newspaper editorials, and NGO press releases finally coalesced to generate a sufficient shift in the political winds to steer the bureaucrats and politicians toward doing the right thing. It would be nice to believe that things work that way, but there are reasons to doubt it.

We can compare Live8 to F15, that day in 2003 when millions of people around the world—at least 14 million, possibly as many as 20 million—took to the streets to protest against the prospect of war in Iraq. The war proceeded anyway, leaving those millions and many more to experience the exhilaration and dismay of genuine dissent against their governments. It became clear then as never before that the ruling powers can treat massive popular protest as a police matter rather than as a crisis of their own legitimacy. The democratic contraptions that are supposed to transform popular discontent into a common project appear to be perpetually out of order.

F15 attempted to stop a war before it started; Live8 aimed to endorse an economic plan that had already been decided by ministers and bureaucrats weeks before. Its value as a political action consisted in the way it elicited pleasure by stating the obvious and enfolding audiences in its apparently painless, frictionless unanimity. The mass mobilization of crowds through media spectacle is fundamentally conservative: it serves purposes defined from the top down, rather than serving as a means of expression from the bottom up. So instead of conceiving of Live8 as a successful effort to flex the political muscles of a nascent televisual constituency, it seems much more plausible to think of the concerts as a "public diplomacy" campaign on behalf of governments—especially the US and the UK, but even including Russia—desperate to appear responsive and humane. Live8 explicitly proposed to its audiences that they were exercising political agency solely by virtue of their inert spectatorship—a role with less expressive force than the audience of *American Idol*. In modern media democracies, a fleeting kind of popular legitimacy can be bought just that cheaply. That is why such events serve as a perfect supplement to the customary exercise of power in advanced consumer societies: by encouraging people to demand what has already been decided for them, governments can issue orders as if there were no alternatives while manufacturing a good public conscience and sense of accomplishment on a mass scale.

Although Live8 took its bearings from Live Aid, played twenty years before, its place in history is much more directly grounded in the events of the past few years. It was staged at the conjuncture of two kinds of crisis, and its success consists in the way it seemed to reconcile them. On one hand, there has been a crisis in the global anticapitalist movement, which has been struggling to regain the momentum it built up after Seattle and Genoa. No doubt much of the popular support for Make Poverty History is drawn from veterans of that movement who saw the campaigns of 2005 as a small step toward more comprehensive changes. (For those interested in the internal politics of NGOs, it would be instructive to trace Bono's own relationship to the Jubilee movement, and explore the reasons why he decided to keep his distance from them, and they from him.) At the same time, on a much different scale, there has been a crisis in the ruling economic orthodoxy, which has seen its own internal doctrinal cohesion falter and its own prescriptions fail. The so-called Washington Consensus, confidently enforced by the IMF, World Bank, and other economic institutions since the 1970s, has been comprehensively challenged from within the ranks of its own practitioners. Now it appears that even die-hard believers in Adam Smith are scrambling to rebuild some semblance of government infrastructure in weakened states throughout the poor world. And thus the time is ripe for a new synthesis. The mission itself—making the world safe for the wealthiest individuals, enterprises, and nations—has not changed, but it has adopted the very same tone of righteousness that its critics once invoked against it.

Jeffrey Sachs wrote *The End of Poverty* in order to rewrite the prescriptions of neoliberal economics in the face of a zealously neoconservative political climate. It represented a rebranding of his shock therapy prescriptions for a new range of patients in the global south. The book's release was timed to coincide with the Gleneagles summit, and it was kitted out with a publicity campaign to maximize its mainstream appeal. The book jacket announces: "Foreword by Bono." Indeed, the foreword effectively rehearses the key themes of the book. First of all, Bono is full of praise for Sachs's expertise and wisdom. Second, he tries to coin catchy slogans that will not only "sell" the argument (like a good pop song) but also make it seem irresistible and inevitable. Let's look at just one key sentence:

Bono says that Sachs proposes an "equation that crosses human with financial capital, the strategic goals of the rich world with a new kind of planning in the poor world."[15] If we accept that slogans matter, it is hard not to be struck by the awkwardness of his phrasing. Even if we accept that all of the world's problems and possibilities should be described in terms of "capital," why would we want to draw an equation between "human" capital and "financial" capital? Instead of balancing the terms, this equation inexorably twists in one direction, recasting fundamental human concerns in the idiom of finance, as if a more rigorously economic approach to global problems would deliver us from the vagaries of politics. Wasn't that the problem with the debt crisis in the first place? And what happens when "the strategic goals of the rich world" are combined with "planning in the poor world"? That is the most damning "equation" of all, wherein the rich world assures its strategic superiority by imposing its own preferred kind of planning. In one respect, Bono's phrasing is exact: the planning will take place "in" the poor world—not by the poor world, nor for it.

It is hard to avoid the impression that the "new paradigm" is essentially the same as the old one, now pursuing global free market restructuring in the name of morality rather than economic efficiency. (If people want to believe that "the right thing to do" will be more efficient and profitable, so much the better.) Weak states might be built up far enough to deliver limited health services and primary education, but not far enough to reclaim sovereign control over their own economic priorities. The same messianic faith in global markets that drove Sachs to prescribe shock therapy for Bolivia, Poland, and Russia is here applied to sectoral aid, trade reform, and an economic triage of the developing world. The prescriptions must be written in such a way that there cannot be, as Sachs would put it, any triumph of politics over economics. (The popular rejection

15   Bono, "Foreword," in Sachs, *The End of Poverty,* p. xv.

of neoliberalism in Bolivia and the oligarchic restoration in Russia strike Sachs as temporary aberrations from the permanent verities of economic science.) Above all Sachs wants to argue that the end of poverty can be accomplished without diminishing, let alone threatening, the accumulation regime organized by the rich world. Thus the accent of guilt has been switched from the past to the future: the rich should no longer feel guilty about the historical processes that brought about impoverishment and suffering, because that had nothing to do with the accumulation of their wealth, but they should henceforth feel responsible for ameliorating the suffering of others, because their security demands it and, in a pinch, their surplus can afford it.

Three and a half months after the Gleneagles G8 summit, where the multilateral debt relief and aid package had been announced, Bono visited the White House again for another photo opportunity. What was the deal this time? On whose behalf does he strike his deals? Who or what does he represent? Does he represent others like himself, well-meaning citizens of the West who feel indignant and guilty over the suffering of the poor and the sick? Or does he represent the poor and the sick themselves, as their self-appointed spokesman and champion? Bono made his position perfectly clear in a *Rolling Stone* interview published just before this meeting with Bush: "I'm representing the poorest and most vulnerable people. On a spiritual level, I have that with me. I'm throwing a punch, and the fist belongs to people who can't be in the room, whose rage, whose anger, whose hurt I represent. The moral force is way beyond mine, it's an argument that has much more weight than I have."[16]

Is that so? By what right does he claim to represent the poorest and most vulnerable people? Does he represent all of them, everywhere around the world? It is hard to know what he could mean by such a statement. Political representation, at least in a democratic key, is

16   Jann Wenner, "Bono: The Rolling Stone Interview," *Rolling Stone*, October 20, 2005. Available online: rollingstone.com

supposed to involve some kind of deliberative process, whereby a group of people choose a representative as their surrogate, advocate, or intercessor. Moreover, this decision to name a representative has to be grounded in the principles of freedom and procedures of sovereignty that govern such acts, so that all parties—including representatives of other people—can accept the legitimacy of the representative. Only through such a process can a representative be considered responsible for and answerable to those people he or she represents. But enough of these technicalities. It is obvious that Bono cannot be the "literal" or "legal" representative of the poorest and most vulnerable people. If he were, he wouldn't be standing in the Oval Office.

Instead, he presents himself as the figurative and spiritual representative of a vast array of people, billions of them. He does not claim to represent their interests, their perspectives, or even their hopes, but rather their "rage, anger, and hurt." That is to say, he does not represent human beings, he represents affects, detached from real lives and filtered through his celebrity image. In his sleepy-eyed seriousness and sympatico slouch—which is the current signifier for "compassion"—he absorbs and deflects everything that those billions of people might actually say on their own behalf. It is not as if "the poorest and most vulnerable people" do not express themselves, in countless ways, all the time. They are articulate, deliberate, and far too various to be summed up just by their pain or their poverty. They have many representatives, too, in and out of governments. All of them are aching to be heard. None of that seems to matter when Bono goes to the White House. Indeed, we should make no mistake about it: he can stand there *precisely because* those people are so absent; he can speak for them exactly insofar as they are silenced; he can "throw a punch" at Bush, Blair, Obama, or any of the others only because he disguises the immense material force of their lives with the soft "moral force" of his rhetoric. The short circuit between imperial power and media spectacle makes every image of Bono—whether at the White House, Davos, Cannes, Ghana, or anywhere else—an apt visualization of the prevailing global order, shuttling between remote-control imperial projection and helping-hand philanthropy. What is missing, invisible, off the agenda, is any belief that economic development can be a mode of collective self-determination, opening up a realm of freedom for the poor beyond that envisioned for them by billionaires.

The trajectory of Bono's campaigns over the past decade tells us a great deal about the limits of philanthropy, reform, and popular politics in a world where any feeling of global collectivity seems increasingly remote. In its earliest phases the debt relief effort drew upon established movements that were challenging longstanding historical injustices; Bono left those behind in order to strike deals with Bush and Blair (among others). As he encountered obstacles, he drove the agenda in wider circles, sweeping up disparate causes into an omnibus program that migrated toward the media main-stream, preferring conservative pieties to progressive abrasion. The Project Red campaign—a series of branding agreements that lever-age symbolic synergies across sneakers, sunglasses, computers, and other aspirational goods—set out to prove that consumerism could trump both old-fashioned charity and official aid. After years of consolidation, the ONE organization (named after a U2 song) now functions as a kind of all-purpose NGO, a shadow UN fuelled by celebrity endorsements and colored wristbands. For a time it seemed as if Bono had succeeded in cornering the market in moral outrage, which he repackaged in a form that could turn a profit and soothe the uneasy heads of state. Yet in spite of his high-flown rhetoric, he does not want to forge a bond of solidarity and obligation between the mass audience he addresses in the West and the subjects in the South whom he claims to represent: such a bond might all too easily turn against the system he serves. Try as he might, he can hardly disguise the fact that the end of poverty will require a radical change in the current order of things. It will require new languages and new images—nothing like anything Bono has to offer.

5   Spaces of Indebtedness

What does indebtedness look like? If being in debt involves something more than a mental state or a legal status, and it necessarily encompasses a range of social relations and productive forces, we should be able to find its traces everywhere, built into our landscape and flashing across our screens. Yet indebtedness does not exactly present itself as such: there is something not quite visible about it, as if the phenomenal world and the people in it could always be measured against their debts and found somehow lacking. It is hard to see indebtedness at work in the world—although it exists nowhere else—precisely because it shows us a world where nothing ever really belongs to itself.

In order to start thinking about the relationship between indebtedness, visibility, and space, we can turn to an essay by Gilles Deleuze, "Postscript on Control Societies" (1990). In this text, one of his last, Deleuze outlines a general historical shift away from the "disciplinary societies," so thoroughly analyzed by Foucault, toward what he wants to call the "control societies" of the present day. Disciplinary societies were defined by "sites of confinement"—prisons, hospitals, factories, schools, the family household—that shaped individuals into mass components of social force: the docile bodies of labor, the patient bodies of the health system, the bodies-in-training of the education system, the oedipalized bodies of the family, and so on. Foucault wanted to grasp the whole program of modernity through these isomorphisms, which had themselves replaced and rationalized the operations of an older model of social power he called the "sovereign society." Each of these successive models—sovereign, disciplinary, control—has its own "machines," its own spatial and temporal forms of organization. The defining machine of the sovereign society was the state apparatus centered on the king's body, invested with natural right from the top down; disciplinary society has its Panopticon, the extension of carceral logic from the penal system outward into all institutions of social conditioning. The question is, What are the defining machines, the decisive sites, the prevailing logics, of the control societies that dominate our own moment?

This is where, in moving beyond Foucault, Deleuze draws a number of tantalizing contrasts: where discipline molds, control modulates; where discipline concentrates, control disperses; whereas discipline uses bureaucratic numbers and personal signatures to fix the identity and relationships of an individual within the mass, control uses coded keycards, electronic tags, and PINs to create shifting layers of mobility and security. The techniques of confinement that characterized disciplinary societies have been reconfigured into the "instant communication" and "continual monitoring" of control societies. As we begin to sort through our own everyday experiences, we may find all kinds of continuity and overlap between the two regimes, especially because surveillance can work even more effectively when people are set loose and left to their own devices. But Deleuze evidently wants to identify a basic operation or technique in "control societies" that could not have been exercised by surveillance and confinement alone. In posing the hypothesis of something radically new, he is not only trying to chart the fault lines in a situation still mixed and in flux, but also seeking to name emergent dangers and the possibilities that necessarily accompany them.

What is distinctively new in control societies? Perhaps most of us would leap to the most obvious answer: information technology, telecommunications networks, digital culture—and Deleuze does indeed cite those features. But he adds something unexpected. He

writes: "Man is no longer the enclosed man, but the indebted man."
[*L'homme n'est plus l'homme enfermé, mais l'homme endetté.*][1]

There are perhaps too many things to say about this line. The key
point hinges on the multivalent distinction between enclosure and
indebtedness, but first we should pause to examine the reasons for
the insistence on the word *man—l'homme*. Here it cannot be read
as the bland generic name for people in general. Instead it marks a
specifically Deleuzian distinction between Man as a single dominant
form of being and the countless ways of escaping that state by becoming otherwise (becoming-woman, becoming-animal, becoming-
imperceptible). In this sense, every appeal to the human—whether in
philosophy, politics, or art—must be seen as a kind of trap, another
way of arresting ourselves by fatally identifying with a transcendent
idea or an ironclad signifier. Much of Deleuze's philosophy turns on
revealing and dissolving the transcendental exception that clings to
the notion of Man and its string of historically variable surrogates.
He never speaks of Man without a tone of antagonism, not because it
is a universalizing concept, but because it is a coercive, reductive, and
exclusionary one. In his later years he often spoke, recalling Primo
Levi, of "the shame of being a human," [*la honte d'être un homme*], a
shame of all the ways, catastrophic and trivial, in which we go along
with the program and thus find ourselves cut off from the chance to
make our own lives. Deleuze's "shame of being human," so different
from the accusing shame of judges and moralists, declares an ethical
refusal of permanent confinement and infinite obligation.

"Enclosure" and "indebtedness," for Deleuze, name two major regimes of social power, two programs of domination, each combining
specific kinds of state authority with distinct economic imperatives and
logics. In the current moment, indebtedness supplements and over-
takes enclosure to become the crucial apparatus of control. Taking this

---

1   Gilles Deleuze, "Postscript on Control Societies," *Negotiations, 1972–1990*, trans.
Martin Joughin (New York: Columbia University Press, 1995), p. 181. See original
edition, *Pourparlers* (Paris; Minuit, 1990), p. 246.

thought as a working hypothesis, there are several questions we might ask. Ideally, we would pause long enough to make an investigation of the way "indebtedness" has haunted contemporary Continental theory, including the deconstructive questioning of responsibility, the recurrent anthropological dream of the unexchangeable gift, the sociological mapping of the social habitus, and the critical examination of the institution of law as a mediation of guilt and violence. It should be possible to find a common thread in these various inquiries, as if each of the human sciences had, at some point in the past few decades, worried over the problem of how subjects and societies might constitute themselves in relationships before or beyond exchange.

But here I want to return to my initial question: what does the current regime of indebtedness *look like*?

Now I think we know what "enclosure" looks like. In its earliest form, "enclosure" produced the topography of capitalist agriculture by throwing people off the land and erasing the commons. At its most basic and brutal stage, enclosure had a long history, legible in hedgerows, property deeds, reciprocal borders, and exclusive legal jurisdictions. Foucault describes a more rigorously rationalized kind of enclosure, homogenizing the largest administrative zones and the tightest spaces of confinement. Its megamachines are clearly still very much with us and won't be going away anytime soon. Yet all the forms and functions of enclosure would need to be reconceived in light of their supersession, beginning with the political models and economic processes that depend on bounded sovereignty and socialized discipline. The prison cell, the schoolroom, the assembly line, the head office, the bureaucratic district, the city limits, the "national economy," the stable work force, and the good citizenry: all of these sites and units, whose consistency depended on being ordered from the inside, are in the process of being dispersed or slivered up on the spot, ready to be reconfigured from the outside.

In fact, architecture has always provided the best visualizations of this regime of social power, from the Panopticon itself, through the various modernist programs for urban autonomy, self-sufficiency, and total planning, all the way to the Twin Towers of the World Trade Center, famously analyzed by Michel de Certeau in *The Practice of Everyday Life* as the monumental "exaltation" of the "scopic drive," the dream of taking command of the city from above, guaranteeing its rational organization, synchronic integrity, and anonymous administration. In fact, de Certeau's analysis of the city presents itself as both an extension of Foucault's critique of totalizing enclosure and as its immanent critique, from below, in the shape of unpredictable and unplanned "practices," a kind of resistance squirreled away in unremarkable gestures and inconspicuous places. We did not need to see the destruction of the WTC to know that de Certeau's critique was incomplete and rather misplaced. (It was hard to avoid the terrible feeling that so many people were killed that day because they just happened to be working inside a monument that had been mistakenly thought to be the irreplaceable symbolic support of American power. Whatever else it was, it was not that.) If de Certeau is right to say that the dominant system of social power lives through a scopic drive, it now seems possible to ask if enclosure, the rationalization and bureaucratization of territory, might have already reached a limit beyond which it cannot go. There is no reason to doubt that the spaces built up according to this model will continue to "work" all by themselves, more or less according to plan. But as soon as the forces they have amassed reach new thresholds—as soon as factories cannot contain the new productive powers, as soon as schools cannot contain the demand for training, as soon as hospitals cannot contain the supervision of health—the model exhausts its capacity to expand in space, and a new dynamics of social relationships, along with a new optics, becomes necessary.

Thus the current regime of indebtedness presents itself as the intensive resumption and redirection of a hitherto extensive process. How does it make itself visible? Aren't we used to thinking of debt as something invisible, internal, even spiritual? Isn't the promise to pay or the promise to believe always something like an attitude or disposition, all the more effective when it does not rely on visible signs and supports?

Yet Deleuze rejects any strictly internalized notion of indebtedness. Of course, long ago Nietzsche's *Genealogy of Morals* insisted that all spiritual debts are written in real blood. Deleuze and Guattari's first book, *Anti-Oedipus* (1972) takes the point further: here we find a sustained treatment of the historical forms of debt, organized in three major configurations. In the first, the so-called "savage" system, debt is incurred and discharged through blood revenge and cruelty; in the "despotic/barbarian" system, all debts are exercised as dispensations of the infinite credit of the divine ruler (it is the latter phases of this system that Foucault will call "sovereign society"); and finally, in the third system, which is capitalism as such, debts finally break free from the authority of the state and circulate across the whole social surface. Inheritance of the past ceases to be collective stockpiling or direct bequest, and instead takes shape as a private accumulation of capital; reciprocal responsibilities cease to be tied to lateral alliances or hierarchical obligations, and instead become subject to oscillating and optional transactions. Henceforth there will be countless ways to be in debt, in all directions and according to various codes and protocols.

Each of these systems, then, produces its own visibility of debt, its own kind of social "eye." Is it really just a metaphor to speak of an "eye" that oversees every group or every society, and places its imprint on every image they make? In every case, the social "eye" would be a kind of collective inscription of memory that keeps track of filiations and alliances, imposes duties, and records payments. In the first system, the memory is inscribed directly on the body, as a mark of pain; in the second, it is decreed by the Law; in the third, it circulates in the flows of money. In each configuration, debt remains primary in relation to institutions of authority, relationships of domination, and circuits of exchange. By this account, Adam Smith's metaphor "the invisible hand" would have to be paired with an "invisible eye" to capture what is new about the capitalist regime: the market-eye keeps a watch over everything, perpetually weighing current values and potential worth; the hand of action and the voice of authority make themselves felt only under the naked light of money. The two great abstract machines that define our era—the market and the media—are two faces of this inscriptive-projective process, the organization of lived temporality around the interminable working-up and working-off of an imperishable indebtedness. "The assault of the present on the rest of time," as Alexander Kluge has put it.

What kind of evidence might give substance to this diagnosis? In keeping with the conceptual pairing of market and media, we might say that the conjuring trick works in two directions, from above and from below: on the one hand, every appearance of value aspires to lift off from its immediate setting, obeying the irresistible pull of global currents; on the other, the immense elsewhere of global markets cannot help but come down to earth in the form of tangible artifacts and the incessant reshaping of built space. Here, then, is the answer to our initial question: the regime of indebtedness makes itself visible only in the parallax of immaterial abstraction and material consumption, crisscrossing between the extremes of spectacular finance and world-historical shopping.

It is not hard to see the sumptuous side of this system. The financial markets continue to be glorified as a combination of spectator sport and online game, while stock trading has been recast as a kind of aesthetic experience. (If once we would never have thought that buying stock in a sugar company could taste sweet, now we cannot be so sure.) There is no doubt that the ever more intimate mixing of capital markets and media apparatuses has a reciprocal effect: a whole repertoire of narrative and affective devices now invest the animal spirits of money with soulful transcendence, while the consumption of media products is supplemented by instant-feedback market satisfactions—watching box office rankings bounce or website hits add up—as if spending money were some kind of investment in a competitive cultural enterprise. And in a very general sense, this compounding of apparatuses is not at all new: "markets" and "media" have been inextricable all along. Markets can be defined as telecommunications systems that pull together territories and populations through commerce, bound by different media of value; and teletechnologies can be understood as deterritorializing mechanisms par excellence, the tools through which everything can be dislodged from the here and now and sent off somewhere else and into another time. Markets and media do not simply complement or duplicate each other: they make and unmake each other all the time, in such a way that all the functions of culture, politics, and economics are continually being reshuffled and redistributed along their axes. Subjectivity itself is constituted by this making and unmaking, caught up in a spiral of belonging: the imperative to amass more and more belongings requires that people belong ever more fully to the apparatus itself.

And yet, as recent events have shown, a capitalism that feeds on the all-encompassing spectacle of wealth can also choke on it. The precariously overleveraged financial sector, riding far beyond the calculus of returns, has suggested, in its very extravagance, a refusal to acknowledge that local or punctual events can any longer interrupt the world time of capital. To forestall any day of reckoning, every effort is being made to persuade us to live into a world nobody can really afford. Fredric Jameson's pointed observation, in his book *Seeds of Time*, that environmental disaster is easier to imagine than the breakdown of capitalism, speaks directly to the way the *longues durées* and sudden eruptions of historical time are henceforth mediated and arbitrated through the market pricing of risk.[2] In the halting implementation of Kyoto, the inevitable ruination of the earth itself is made subject to shrewd calculations of profit and cost, where the opening of a market in the rights to spoil the land, sea, and air is supposed to count as

---

2   Fredric Jameson, *Seeds of Time* (New York: Columbia University Press, 1995), p. xii. See also "The Brick and the Balloon: Architecture, Idealism and Land Speculation," in *The Cultural Turn* (London: Verso, 1998), for a bold theorization of the linkages between financial speculation and architectural aesthetics.

some kind of progress. What we see here is in fact the codification of a further kind of indebtedness—a kind of reverse ecology—in which all-encompassing economic institutions set the terms whereby nature and humankind will pay for their own survival. We come to realize with a feeling of dread that the sudden collapse of capitalist structures would be environmentally catastrophic: as David Harvey has argued, the history of "continuous human action" upon the world's ecosystems has gone on long enough that even a brief interruption would bring dire consequences. Human intervention has so thoroughly reorganized the global ecosystem that this system now depends on our supervision, even as it becomes ever more vulnerable to our exploitation.[3]

By the time it becomes possible to imagine the enlistment of the earth into the "full body" of indebtedness, the concept has clearly reached some kind of outer limit. Yet this orbiting perspective is exactly what media discourse offers: the point of view from which it appears that each of us can make decisions on a planetary scale. As we've seen in an earlier chapter, the profuse circulation of images and information is framed by a "strategic" presentation of any and every situation. (That is equally true, whether the question is whether you should buy Microsoft or bomb Iraq.) It is easy to say that the "strategic" perspective is a perfectly cynical pose, from Fox and CNBC on down. But it is more plausible to say that this scheming calculating eye is an indispensable aspect of media subjectivity, coupled with the utter lack of effective means to act on what we see, except for regulated moves in the game of passive acquiescence. This is what Deleuze and Guattari mean when they say that capitalism operates schizophrenically, through a disconnection between hand, voice, and eye. The film *A Beautiful Mind* celebrates this disconnection in just these terms: the man credited with formalizing the logic of market relations in game theory turns out to be a schizo who breaks under

---

3   David Harvey, "What's Green and Makes the Environment Go Round?" in *Cultures of Globalization*, ed. Fredric Jameson and Masao Miyoshi (Durham: Duke University Press, 1998).

the overload of American media. The two mental states—each one grasping for a total truth—only accidentally inhabit the same body. What the film does not ask is whether it takes a real schizo to grasp the functioning of markets, or to take a distance from the operations of media power. There is certainly something schizophrenic about living amid the phantasmagoria of wealth. Having presupposed the dominion of the system in order to strategize our way around in it, we can then reward ourselves by becoming sovereigns of our own personal space. That's what shopping is for.

Unlike the buildings and cityscapes that owe their existence to the recent burst of financial speculation, the contemporary spaces of shopping might not seem especially distinctive. Quite the contrary: shopping spaces run the gamut from the most high-tech specialty stores to the most familiar junk spaces just down the street. That is why everybody seems to have developed such fine-tuned psycho-geographic instincts about shopping space: you know in an instant where you belong and where you do not, even though all shopping spaces are supposed to be open to anybody with cash or credit. The default organization of such spaces emphasizes access and transparency, turning the simple acts of walking and looking around into a series of encounters between shopper and merchandise. In essence, shopping spaces produce enclosure, plus a vector of movement. In the opening pages of the massive *Harvard Design School Guide to Shopping*—surely the most definitive recent document on the subject—we can see a rough evolution from the souks of Isfahan and arcades of Paris to the Crystal Palace of London and the Southdale of Edina, Minnesota: in each venue there is a mall-like floor space capped by a more or less ornate light-giving roof.[4] The larger argument of this remarkable book, however, is that shopping space has been mutating and migrating: the authors calculate that there is a global average of four square feet of retail space per person. (In the

---

4   Chuihua Judy Chung, Jeffrey Inaba, Rem Koolhaas, Sze Tsung Leong, eds., *Harvard Design School Guide to Shopping* (Köln: Taschen, 2001).

US, as always the world leader, there are thirty-one square feet per person.[5]) Even more than the sprawling subdivisions or the half empty skyscrapers, the sheer proliferation of shopping spaces should be seen as the physical extension of the regime of indebtedness, where individual subjects are empowered to enact their own fidelity to the reigning powers of money. Shopping embraces the basic contradiction of consumerism, offering a way to bear being in debt, turning endless obligation into fleeting enjoyment, staking a claim in a collective excess that would be inaccessible to mere individuals.

The *Guide to Shopping* was assembled by a research team associated with the Dutch architect Rem Koolhaas. The lessons of the project were filtered immediately into the designs produced by Koolhaas's firm, the Office for Metropolitan Architecture (OMA), for a series of shopping spaces for the Italian fashion company Prada. The New York Prada store, dubbed an "epicenter," was opened in 2001, and a second "epicenter" in Los Angeles was opened in 2004. (The preparatory materials for these and other projects were published in a volume titled *Projects for Prada*.[6] OMA has also published a volume of material related to its designs for art exhibition space for the Prada Foundation.) For better and for worse, it is no exaggeration to say that Koolhaas's designs for Prada present the most concentrated and most thoroughly contemporary shopping spaces available. More than that, an analysis of the Koolhaas/Prada projects shows how contemporary architecture might offer some kind of figurative presentation of the global processes implied by the notion of indebtedness, just as older regimes of power produced distinctive architectures of their own (the sovereign Baroque, for example, or, again, the Panopticon itself). But now we have to wonder: does power—insofar as it passes over into networks of economic circuitry—make itself visible that way anymore? Is it possible to register (if not to represent) the global sprawl of an indebted world within the terms of a single building?

5   *Ibid.*, p. 51.
6   Rem Koolhaas, *Projects for Prada, Volume 1* (Milan: Fondazione Prada Edizioni, 2001).

Koolhaas organizes his designs around a series of physical and imaginary encounters between shoppers and the corporate entity of Prada. At every turn those encounters are structured by solicitations, negotiations, and obligations. On the shopper's side, the encounter is initiated by a space marked as the "street"—"where customers can visit Prada without the obligation to buy"—which cuts from the sidewalk outside to the entrance area inside. This offer of hospitality is startling not so much for its generosity, but because it alerts us to the question: how does a space or an image ever impose an obligation to buy? At what point do the shopper's desires manifest themselves as a demand coming from the merchandise itself, as an order that has to be obeyed? On Prada's side, Koolhaas writes, "Prada has aura without obligation. It is not burdened by one inflexible image." Here we can ask: how can Prada claim the aura of its past without also reproducing it in the future? What kind of promise or guarantee is embodied in everything it sells? On one hand, we have the shopping spectator, eager to be captivated; on the other, the attractive and elusive seller, whose unanswerability forms an essential element of its allure. In the midst of this ambiguous relationship, then, Koolhaas presents his design as a way to forgive debts: relieving the shopper from the obligations that Prada might demand and relieving Prada of its history, allowing it to inherit its own past simply by making it new. Koolhaas, or architecture, as intercessor—it is a beautiful and ingenious approach. Of course, it is a trick: neither Prada nor the shopper is actually off the hook; otherwise, there would be no reason to invest so much money in preparing a place for the two to meet.

That is why the design must also impose debts of a very special kind. The shopper will be addressed in several ways: as the actual subject of architectural luxury (Prada will lavish its costly space on her) and as the potential subject of service (in exchange for an implicit promise to buy, Prada will draw her into deeper intimacies, until the transaction itself appears as inessential as possible). The shopper's passage from being treated and respected as an anonymous member of the public to being received as a special friend may take just an instant. Surveillance and identification has become a mutual, even an intimate, compact: Koolhaas projects a system where shoppers will carry electronic Prada ID cards, and the staff will wield scanners to keep track of the intricate dance of people and commodities. The store offers the customer all the space she needs to pretend that the desire to belong to Prada can really be satisfied by a discrete purchase.

In order to intensify the passage from passive onlooker to passionate consumer, Koolhaas codifies a range of more and less accessible spaces in the floor plan itself. The most striking feature of the New York store—a giant wave scooped out of the floor, configured as a performance stage/shoe display—seems like an extravagant gift to the public, drawing crowds in to gawk at the wasted floor space. Tucked away in the basement, the elaborate dressing rooms offer the opposite kind of luxury, a zone of privacy that is simultaneously shut off from the outside and immediately accessible to service. Here is an enclosure made of light and glass, a teletechnology built around the body, a Panopticon in reverse perspective: it includes a door that can be made transparent or opaque at the touch of a button; a "magic mirror" that is really a camera, projecting one's image from different angles, with variable time lags; and finally, a phone "like a prison phone," for communicating with people outside. The plans also call for VIP rooms, special "clinic" and "library" sections, and secret entrances; in these deeper enclaves, the relationship of commercial obligation is meant to disappear, so that the shopper is able to play a variety of other roles in partnership with Prada. Throughout the documents, Koolhaas emphasizes experimentation and research, as if the shopper will have a chance to anticipate the objects that will renew the bonds between customer and brand.

For its part, Prada is freed from the obligation to be itself, to repeat itself, or even to have a corporate presence, beyond the one fabricated as "aura." Its "stability," according to the Glossary, is achieved by "a system of continuous innovation." At the level of the store, this dynamism is signaled not only by the architectural elements (the wallpaper, the media stage) or the commodities on sale, but especially by the media components scattered throughout the store: the website console, the "peep show" room filled with small LCDs flashing a variety of images, and the "triptych" panels "where the more religiously inclined Prada customer can commune with the Prada aura in an intimate and immersive manner." Clearly, the "aura" generated here accrues as much to the teletechnologies as to the Prada corporation. Because the "content" of the media flows constantly changes, the Prada aura (as opposed to Prada commodities) remains strictly inaccessible to any particular store visitor: all we can see is its profusion. In contrast to those peer brands that aim for exclusivity by rationing their public and private faces (for example, the John Pawson design for Calvin Klein), Koolhaas asks Prada to stake its identity on the way it can afford to squander images, scramble circuits, and invite noise into its home. (It is worth noting here that Koolhaas had originally hoped to open a Prada subway station below the store.)

That is not to say that the Prada store in New York becomes, in pursuit of aura, something entirely given over to the public. Somewhere between intimate service and public hospitality, the shopper will encounter some resistance, and she must decide whether or not to give in. In fact, the design is filled with the trappings of enclosure: there are looming cages fitted on overhead tracks, the so-called hanging city; the blackened reception booths overlook passages in and out; and of course, the "Prada army" of well-dressed staff roam everywhere, augmented by less well dressed security guards we should call Prada police. Somewhere the "regimes of freedom" set loose in the store come up against their "container": sooner or later everyone has to buy something or be chased away. Koolhaas offers a remarkable formulation for this process: the store "captures attention and hands it back to the consumer." Or again: "We give people the freedom not to shop." The sovereign aura of Prada binds and releases the shopper, so that the shopper's exercise of free choice and self-fashioning serves as a return gift to Prada for its generosity. How does Prada compel such an exchange? Can it ever afford to suspend the imperative to make people spend money in its store? If we believe Koolhaas, that is the wrong way to look at it: instead of drawing the anonymous customer deeper into its clutches, the Prada store, as "epicenter," does everything to expel its claim on our attention outward, past the threshold, onto the street and into the world.

Even on its small scale, the Prada store registers something of the extra-large economic circuitry that characterizes our moment. Nevertheless it tries to bear this weight lightly. The streams of images and the sockets of information can be found tucked in corners, hanging from racks, or lying casually on tabletops. And even if many of the most characteristic image and data flows of our age can be seen crossing through here—everything from fashion's eternal flashes to the stubbornly uneventful shots of security gates, loading docks, and empty shop floors—this media assemblage does not attempt to offer a separate vantage point from which we might say what the shop or the company "means." Instead, the images show no more and no less than other places and other times upon which this particular moment somehow depends; those moments may be as "real" as a surveillance camera or as "unreal" as a Pasolini seduction, as familiar as a catwalk snippet or as unfamiliar as a Lagos traffic jam, but Prada somehow depends on all of them.

Likewise we should take the maps presented at the beginning of *Projects for Prada* seriously. They plot the deployment of Prada stores around the world, superimposed on notations of population, climate, GDP, and national debt. One need only compare the GDP and national debt maps to get the point: on the first, where countries are drawn larger or smaller in proportion to their share of world GDP, the green Prada squares dominate the mass of the world; on the second, where whole continents are crossed off because they are trapped under their debts, Prada's outposts cling to the edges of the world. Because the less indebted countries are colored in the same green as the Prada markers, one might be tempted to draw the conclusion that Prada stores somehow displace the burden of debts worldwide. Which comes first, Prada or national prosperity? Which comes first, Prada or individual desire?

It has often been suggested that fashion stands in relation to ordinary items in something like the way speculative capital stands toward productive capital. While the latter is engaged in the useful work that keeps everything going, the former seems to push one step ahead, put one foot in the future. As Simmel and Benjamin saw it, fashion acquired an aspect of timelessness exactly because it wagered everything on its transience. (The glossy magazines, with perfect cynicism, attribute this timelessness to individual people, and call it "style." Thus they flatter the reader by pretending that the goods on display are merely fashionable accoutrements to a personal quality, when in fact objects alone are the essential element, bearing the mark of glamour as the imprint of the system.) Koolhaas's work on the Prada store transposes this dynamic into spatial terms. It is not that the store is supposed to transport shoppers into the future, but rather that it enlarges the ordinary context of transactions and, at its best, makes visible the more or less sloppy seams suturing mere stuff to the allure of capital.

This fusion of information overload, pleasurable disorientation, and gratuitous luxury presents the act of shopping as the only suitably contemporary way to live in the moment. And at the beginning, anyway, this strategy seemed to be working. Prada sales in the first two months of 2002 outstripped the GDP growth in the US and (by an even wider margin) Japan. But the question remains whether the reported $40 million cost of the store was ultimately aimed at the calculus of sales and profits. Is aura really worth so much money? It is more plausible that the investment was aimed elsewhere: not at consumers but at high finance. Prada had been planning to take its stock public, and hinted that it might launch the IPO sometime in the summer of 2002, a few months after the opening of the New York store. Having run up massive debts expanding its operations through the 1990s, the Prada holding company (almost entirely owned by Miuccia Prada and her husband) aimed to fix its balance sheets and cash in on its ascent to the heights of fashion. But the company retreated from that stock offering, as it has done several times since, balking at the prospect of selling its aura too cheaply. Nevertheless it has found the financing to expand aggressively, including the construction of the "epicenter" stores in Aoyama (designed by Herzog & de Meuron) and Los Angeles (designed by Koolhaas). Indeed, Koolhaas's firm, OMA, has continued to produce "research" materials, design exhibitions, and even catwalks for Prada and its subsidiary labels. At what point does an architectural practice become a brand manager, marketing expert, and iconography specialist? Could it be that the architect's symbolic labor over the company's "exclusivity" and "intrigue" is addressed not so much to actual customers as to potential investors, who may never set foot in any of its stores?

It may well be that shopping is "arguably the last remaining form of public activity," as the OMA website claims. But that is not because it preserves common uses of space or collective forms of experience. On the contrary, shopping might be considered the newest and most contagious form in which the utterly privatized experiences of consumerism make themselves visible. It is not simply a matter of converting hitherto open or public spaces, up for grabs to anybody passing through, into concession stands and advertising surfaces. The more profound changes involve the reorganization of whole landscapes by the newer commercial uses, the wars of position between big-box retail zones, quickly hacked-out commercial strips, and repeatedly reconverted urban neighborhoods. Changing at the speed of local shopping preferences and plugged into the tremors of every macroeconomic boom and bust, the built environment becomes as durable as money and as disposable as the items on sale in the stores. No doubt shopping aspires to envelop the environment, the whole world zoned for "mixed use," a chunk of retail added to everything. In a world built upon the conversion of necessities and luxuries into debts, shopping spaces function as the magnetic poles where each movement of everyday life can be drawn toward the possibility of exchange. Between the need to keep the system going, the requirement to service obligations already incurred, and the insistent demand for more, the present moment never quite gets around to keeping any promises or fulfilling any wishes, and so has none to offer. That is how tomorrow will go, too, if catastrophe doesn't claim it first.

But in the end Deleuze does not see things that way. Immediately after he has indicated the place of indebtedness in the contemporary situation, he goes on to say: "It's true that one thing hasn't changed—capitalism still keeps three-quarters of humanity in extreme poverty, too poor for debt, too numerous for confinement; control will have to deal not only with vanishing frontiers, but with the explosions of shantytowns and ghettos." Here the topography of above and below is fundamentally recast. Even the infinity and intensity of debt is revealed to be a partial, incomplete construction. Its machinery for the absorption of living labor and the exhaustion of creative anticipation cannot finally grasp the full potency of time. This is perhaps the best way to understand what Deleuze understands by "the virtual." Insofar as indebtedness taps into everything people have in common—the uncaptured and undiminished past, and the always energetic renewal of the future—it touches upon the virtual as the living force of the present. Whatever allows us to recognize and realize this amplitude of time, whatever races a little ways ahead, or stays a little while behind, without being immediately recaptured, can show us how to leave the circuits and cycles of capital. It is only in the experience of the insistence of indebtedness that one can keep faith with the need to be rid of it, and the desire to construct different bonds in common.

6   The Magic of Debt; or, Reading Marx Like a Child

Every few years, one of the big media outlets—a network news channel, the *Wall Street Journal*, or the *New Yorker*—will run a splashy think piece about the surprisingly contemporary relevance of Karl Marx. The article, invariably delivered in a bemused and condescending tone, will reveal that Marx actually admired capitalism in some ways, which means that he might have been right about a few things; meanwhile, his trenchant criticisms of it will be treated as the quaintly perceptive observations of an awkward crank. The moral of the story is always the same: Marx has a great deal to teach us about capitalism, but only if we remember that he was wrong.

I want to argue that Marx does indeed have a lot to teach us, especially if we bypass all of the usual rituals of disinterment and reanimation. Echoing an earlier call to arms, I want to suggest that it is time to read Marx again, to the letter. But instead of returning to the most famous texts, I will offer a reading of what might be considered Marx's great undiscovered masterpiece, a missing text that throws unexpected light on the contemporaneity of his work. This text must be counted as one of Marx's most innovative and prolific works, composed on a truly epic scale. But, sadly, it is quite lost to us: we have only a brief secondhand trace of it, rendered in the words of Marx's youngest daughter, Eleanor, who describes how her father, nicknamed "Moor," entertained the family during their long walks around London. Here it is:

He told stories to my sisters during the walks—I was still small—and these stories were divided up not into chapters, but into miles. The two girls would stretch it out by saying "Tell us one more mile." That memory stays with me, so much did I love all the countless wonderful stories that Moor told me, most of all the stories of Hans Röckle. They lasted months and months, because it was one long, long story and it never ended. Hans Röckle was a magician, the kind Hoffmann was fond of, who had a toyshop and many debts. In his shop were the most wonderful things: wooden men and women, giants and dwarves, kings and queens, masters and apprentices, four-footed animals and birds as plentiful as in Noah's Ark, and tables and chairs, carriages and chests great and small. But alas! although he was a magician, he was all the same constantly stuck in money troubles, and so, against his will, he had to sell all his pretty things—piece by piece—to the devil. But after many, many adventures and mishaps these things always came back to Hans Röckle's shop. Some of these adventures were terrible and hair-raising like Hoffmann's tales, others were comical, but all were told with an inexhaustible wealth of inventiveness, imagination, and humor.[1]

That is all there is, but it is more than enough. We will try to recover something more from it than a biographical anecdote. In fact, I think it would be possible to read these adventures as a sketch for a suitably childlike version of *Capital*, encompassing volumes one, two,

---

1   Eleanor Marx-Aveling, untitled excerpt in *Gespräche mit Marx und Engels*, ed. Hans Magnus Enzensberger (Frankfurt: Suhrkamp, 1981), pp. 270–1. Eleanor goes on to testify to Marx's taste for the *Niebelunglied*, Gudrun, Don Quixote, *Thousand and One Nights*, Shakespeare, Walter Scott, Balzac, and Fielding. Elsewhere, Eleanor tells a story about Marx pawning his wife Jenny's heirloom silver and being hassled by the police because the pieces looked too good for a strange foreigner to be peddling [*Gespräche,* pp. 240–1]. This anecdote seems especially relevant here, suggesting that the Hans Röckle stories are, most immediately, fantastic justifications for a father pawning the family's treasures: the stories treat pawning as an adventure, sealed with the guarantee that the pledge will be redeemed and the object will come home again.

and three—the very texts Marx was writing in the years he was telling the stories of Hans Röckle to his daughters.

Let me begin by distinguishing three levels in the story, around which we can organize our reading. First, there is the description of Marx (the old Moor) and his children taking their walks all over London, a German family in exile, quite poor but obviously enjoying themselves. Eleanor recalls nostalgically the pleasures of storytelling in family life. (She also relates that her father often read aloud to the children: "Shakespeare was our house bible.") We should underline the detail that the tales are measured in miles, as though it were the purpose of storytelling to traverse territory, to cut through it or occupy it using the charms of fantasy and narrative. And although we can only guess that the closure of each episode or tale coincides with the family's (and the toys') return home, it seems clear that these stories belong out in the world and that, in their telling, they would have incorporated the living surroundings witnessed by the Marxes in their wanderings. Indeed, the family, again like the toys, are forced to travel as strangers through unknown territory. We know that these walks were famously long, stretching from Soho to the far end of Hampstead Heath, and every mile of storytelling would have crossed a giant slice of the social world. In our study of this picture, we might also speculate on why Eleanor makes a point of saying that the stories were addressed to, and extended by, her sisters, although in the next sentence she claims that the stories were told to her. Given the intense web of patriarchal authority and loyal identification in the Marx family, it is not surprising to find that the addressee of such stories is subtly fractured.

The next level is the story of Hans Röckle, the perennially impoverished magician who traffics with the devil. This core story serves as a wonderfully simple framing device: with a minimum of elements, it outlines a situation out of which many more stories will flow. Eleanor explicitly relates Hans Röckle to the sorcerers in E. T. A. Hoffmann's tales (such as "The Golden Pot"), but Goethe's Faust is clearly here as well, reviewing his own treasures before Mephistopheles comes along to tempt him. And yet there is something rather modern about Röckle's situation and predicament, a combination of great creative power and fundamental helplessness, to which we will return in a moment.

Finally, on the third level, there are the (missing) stories of the toys themselves, the stories that were actually being told on those family walks. It is striking that the toys seem to be the primary narrative actants, serving as both the subjects and the objects of their peculiar destinies. Just as there are many kinds of toys, so there must have been a wealth of narrative genres, as though each toy not only deserved its own tale, but perhaps its own kind of tale, in which the only structural requirement was its eventual return to the toy shop.

The most immediate connection to familiar Marxist territory is here: the toys are recognizably like commodities, expropriated from the one who makes them and sent out to travel a long (but never infinite) chain of transactions before they can be allowed to resume their unremarkable existence as objects of use or enjoyment. Of course, Marx begins the first volume of *Capital* with his analysis of the commodity and its fetishism, showing how the apparently inert objects of social life are in fact dynamic elements of an expansive economic process. Here the hypothesis of fetishism is vividly recast as a fairy-tale trauma: the objects made for pleasure and play are forced to play the game of value, undergoing the hazards of the economic world, before being brought back to the shop, where they come to rest. In this scenario, fetishism is the unhappy enchantment of the enchantment: a disguise that something playful is required to wear in order to pass as a worldly character.

In the list of toys, among all the usual fantastic items, there are one or two conspicuously mundane things, including a box and a table—but even these have special resonance if we recall the celebrated "dancing table" of that first chapter of *Capital*, described in the most surreal fashion by Marx to show how commodities seem to have a material and mystical life of their own. The toys, of course, do indeed have lives of their own, as "wonderful" and "fantastic" as any commodity. But are they fetishes? In *Capital*, the "secret" of the commodity is its "form," the commodity-form itself, more precisely a form of value, the materialization of social relations in a visible, tangible form that allows exchange to occur. In fact, the value-form not only makes exchange possible, it makes it necessary and in some sense *obligatory*, another point to which we will return later.

If the toys harbor any secrets, they are secrets not of work but of play, an activity that is uniquely able to remake the world in its own image. The world of play should not be mistaken for an eruption of the archaic or preeconomic past, or for the humble domain of use-value. If play makes a world, it cannot be a world elsewhere, a fabulous beyond, but just the contrary: it will be a world composed out of materials from the one we think we know. Let us look more closely at the list of toys in Hans Röckle's shop. We have human and animal figures; mythical and monstrous creatures; royalty, masters, and servants; everyday furniture; and vehicles and things to be carried in them. All of these are "wonderful" and "pretty." Their existence as toys in the toyshop is explicitly contrasted to their existence as objects of diabolical exchange, as if the toys exercised their own kind of playful craftiness in order to swim against the tide of exchange and return to Röckle's shop. For as long as the toys remained in the shop, they could be enjoyed only as part of a closed fantasy world; but as soon as they are forced to make their own way—"one by one"—they become playful and fantastic in another sense, as alien agents in a world that seems threatening and controlling. On one hand, the toyshop is Playland, the atemporal origin and destination of all adventures, and on the other hand there is History, the structured domain of narrative and exchange. The toys are thus doubly marvelous: not only do they duplicate the world outside in playful form, but also they proceed to function within that world in the most serious way, even ultimately triumphing over it.

It should not be surprising that Marxist theorists like Benjamin, Adorno, and Bloch have taken a special interest in play and in toys. According to Giorgio Agamben, who follows in this lineage here, "The essence of a toy . . . is an eminently historical thing: it is, so to speak, the Historical in its pure state. For in the toy, as in no other site, can we grasp the temporality of history in its purely differential and qualitative value."[2] For Agamben, the toy is defined by the way it refuses to belong either to the realm of the sacred or to the realm of the practical-economic—dimensions of social life that are thus simultaneously preserved, projected, and cancelled by the toys themselves. Agamben offers a striking suggestion: whereas we have come to think of commodities under the sign of death—as dead labor—and the commodity-form as a kind of ghost or specter that haunts the products of capitalism, we should rather see the toy under the sign of birth—it allows the act of production to be perceived as a kind of reproduction, capable of creating its own fortunes. By enacting this unsettling of temporality, this undecidability of the living and the dead, the toy lets us slip away from both the imperious presence of the metaphysical and the raw presence of the necessary, which together seem to circumscribe every attempt to live.[3]

But by conjuring both indebtedness and inventiveness—combining what is *unwillingly endured* with what is *willingly imagined*—the toy travels a path of the fullest historicality, illuminating what can be brought to life and what has already passed away, and along the way it signals a persistent possibility, the very one promised by Marx, that our lives could be formed freely in history, without surrendering either to the unanswerable sovereignty of what came before or to the implacable exigencies of naked survival.

---

2   Giorgio Agamben, *Infancy and History: On the Destruction of Experience*, trans. Liz Heron (London: Verso, 1993), p. 71.

3   Adorno also speaks of the utopian element of toys. As he puts it in *Minima Moralia*: "The unreality of games [and toys] gives notice that reality is not yet real. Unconsciously they rehearse the right life." (London: Verso, 1974), p. 228.

A first provisional conclusion might be reached here: the stories that Marx told his daughters constitute a pedagogy of play, a lesson in the proper use of things, whereby we learn to release the narrative resources embedded in them precisely in order to overcome an impossible situation.[4] In our little text, the enormous wealth of Marx's stories, from the amazing and frightening to the comic, springs from a simple pattern: the toys leave the shop for some incomprehensible reason, undergo all kinds of "adventures and mishaps," and then return. But why do the toys *have to leave* and why do they *always come back*? Does this inevitability spoil the adventure, serving only to restore order and recapture the outbreak of play? How can there always be a happy ending in the face of such a diabolical situation?

To answer these questions, which casually touch upon the most crucial political issues at stake in Marx, we cannot remain on the level of the toy stories. We have to move back to the second level, to the figure of Hans Röckle and the framing story, in order to see what drives this fabulous economic and narrative machinery. Seen from this angle, the wondrous return of the toys has nothing circular about it, because their course is not governed by any law of exchange or genre. That is to say: because the toys are neither sacred nor practical, they have no destination and no end; their departure signals an inexplicable force and their return signifies instead a kind of wish-fulfillment, forcing us to think through an impossibility we could not express or resolve in any other way. And this wish arises from the unending predicament of Hans Röckle. We could even call it an existential and world-historical predicament. He is no mere worker, no alienated proletarian, but a magician. Yet for all his power, this magician finds himself at the mercy of powers stronger than his own. It is important to stress that Röckle's magical craft is not at all the same kind of magic Marx attributes to capital in his economic writings.

4 The idea that Marx teaches us how to play with narrative has been proposed by Alexander Kluge, who treats it as the salient creative dimension of Marx's work.

Capital is metaphysical in a spectacular way, claiming divine power for the meanest scrap of gold or paper; Hans Röckle's work seems closer to the kind of peasant magic intuited by Benjamin, a "mimetic faculty" that persists, somehow or other, in the face of, indeed at the very heart of, an economic system to which it does not fully belong. With the figure of Hans, we see how the production of "magic" generates a social energy that the word *labor* can no longer convey, yet this energy is something that capitalist processes still cannot do without: the devilish "enchantments" of value need and use the playful magic of production, which can demonstrate its greater powers only when its products, the toys, have put themselves at risk in the profane world of commerce.

Benjamin describes this world-making magic as "the gift [*Gabe*] of producing similarities," which, even if it is exercised by an individual, must be matched by "the gift of recognizing [similarities]" exercised by others. These reciprocal gifts are not things, but collective *capacities* and *dispositions*, which are not only historically variable but also, for Benjamin, historically threatened.[5] It is important to locate "mimesis" as an action performed by Hans rather than a quality possessed by the toys: it is through the contagious correspondences generated by the mimetic faculty that the toymaker somehow takes possession of the world by making toys, and it is this possession we reenact in play. And even though Röckle's toys are taken away from him, they are a crafty kind of gift, a *pharmakon*: offerings that may be both enlivening and poisonous to the order that tries to appropriate them. In the obstinate attitude of the toymaker we find a second lesson: Marx teaches his children to

---

5   Walter Benjamin, "Über das Mimetische Vermögen," *Angelus Novus* (Frankfurt: Suhrkamp, 1966), pp. 96–9; "On the Mimetic Faculty," *Reflections* (New York: Schocken, 1978), trans. Edmund Jephcott, pp. 333–6. What threatens the mimetic is the "semiotic," the primacy of language, and the ordering powers of writing: in the present context, we would have to ask just how capitalism uses writing to impose its debts, and further, how, for Benjamin, writing itself incurs a historical and ineffaceable debt to the mimetic faculty.

celebrate the magician's labor, which harbors the wish that someday all the things crowding our world might, against all appearances to the contrary, be animated by a kind of restorative or redemptive playfulness.

Yet Hans Röckle's situation is not a paradise of innocence and freedom to which we (or the Marx family) might return. We hear the halt in Eleanor's voice: Röckle is a magician, yes, but there is something else, alas. He is described as someone who "has" two things: the toyshop and "many debts." Not one before the other: no toys without debts, and vice versa. It is as if Marx is insisting to his children: if you thought you could have toys without money troubles, you're sadly mistaken. Röckle's whole predicament is money itself: not simply that he does not have enough money, but rather, the fact that *there is money* is a fatal challenge to him. And this threat, this crisis—Eleanor's word is *Geldnöten*, which could mean not only a "shortage" of money, but also the "danger" or "misery" of money— can never be dispelled by magic. The perpetual presence of money, which is therefore also a perpetual absence, takes the form of *debt*, which casts a powerful spell of its own.

Like an obscure curse, Röckle's "many debts" arise spontaneously and never go away. They have nothing directly to do with the devil, who seems to be no more than a middle-class Mephistopheles stepping in to take advantage of another's distress. The devil does not create the debt, but through his mediation he enforces and reinforces it, allowing Hans to defer the final reckoning without ever letting him off the hook. In other words, the devil is just the middleman, not the cause of trouble; without him, Hans would lose everything, but through him every thing is lost anyway, put at risk and drawn into a helpless circulation. This is the child's next real lesson: we are born into this kind of debt, and it will never go away. (Note that the German word for "debt" and "guilt" is the same: *die Schuld*. Not only Nietzsche but also Benjamin probed this polysemy on several occasions.) So if the adventures of the toys are just so many imaginary resolutions to this real situation, the promise of happiness can be won only by a passage through the experience of indebtedness. No matter how improbable the return and restitution may be, and no matter how often it happens, debt will continue to exercise its disruptive pull. That is the devilish thing about it: it may appear external and temporary—an episodic "fact of life"—yet it absorbs, overshadows, and outlasts everything that life can muster against it.

If Röckle's toys can be recognized as magical exiles in the world of commodities, threatened and hopeful at the same time, what can we make of Röckle's debts? If, at the level of the framing device, these debts seem to be no more than a circumstantial presupposition for the stories that follow, can it nevertheless be said that debt becomes—only at a certain historical moment, perhaps—an indispensable component of both economy and narrative? The story seems to teach us that having "money trouble" makes it impossible to be either practically self-sufficient or morally uncompromised. And if that is so, is it possible to imagine another way of living?

To give these questions some theoretical weight, we have to leave Moor and his story behind (for the moment), and ask about Karl Marx. Is there in fact a concept of debt in Marx's economic and social theory? If "debt" were simply a secondary or technical aspect of a more fundamental operation—if it were contained, for example, within the dynamics of exchange or circulation (in the case of finance) or within the sphere of production itself—there would be no need to look for a concept of it. But perhaps it is a fundamental problem for both Moor, who cannot tell a story without it, and Marx, who has trouble defining it.

Here I will have to take a shortcut. To assemble a full definition of debt, one would need to address philosophies of morality and justice and anthropologies of sacrifice and potlatch, as well as the political economy of capitalism, where we could trace the evolution of debt through various financial "revolutions" from the seventeenth century up to the present.[6] As distinct from these broad theoretical and historical lineages, I want to sketch out a specifically Marxist account of debt. I want to propose that the concept of indebtedness articulates *the historicity of life*, that is, life insofar as it becomes social and is lived in common.[7] Such a concept in no way designates something universal and timeless; indeed, thinking about indebtedness should lead us to wonder how it is that debts seem to structure all the time in the world, and whether our historical situation can be grasped only when we try to take all of our debts into account, and finally whether all our ideas of "history" or "the world" are not, before all else, debts we take on (or not) in every act of thinking.

Turning to the key works of Marx, then, one thing is immediately striking: the word *debt* plays no key role in the articulation of his theory. Most often it appears joined to, and eclipsed by, the word *credit*, which is, as I hope to show, *not at all* the other side of the same coin.

Let me propose that there are three distinct aspects or moments in Marx's treatment of what I am calling indebtedness: first, a philosophical dimension, most clearly approached in the early works; second, a full-blown economic dimension, to be found in the *Grundrisse* and the first and second volumes of *Capital*; and finally, a political, perhaps even Utopian, dimension, opened up in *Capital*, Volume 3.

---

6   Alongside all the classical references from Bataille and Benveniste, one should mention David Graeber's excellent summary of the anthropological evidence, "Debt: the First Five Thousand Years," *Mute* magazine, February 10, 2009. Available online: metamute.org. And any survey of the new literature of debt will certainly have to include Margaret Atwood's suggestive book of essays *Payback: Debt and the Shadow Side of Wealth* (Toronto: Anansi Press, 2008).

7   In other words, *debt* names something basic to the experience of social being as a dimension of historicity, even in its most eschatological form: it is the way one acknowledges, *retroactively*, the passage of time to which one henceforth is subject. And so the most absolute kind of debt, original sin, appears as the most foolproof way to give meaning, *proleptically*, to one's death, an act that thus becomes a way to ensure that one's debts will never be paid except by the God who granted them.

Marx's earliest extended treatment of creditors and debtors can be found in an 1844 critique of James Mill. Here Marx employs his most speculative language to lift the problem from the practical to the grandiose: he traces the evolution of the credit and banking system as a progressive alienation of human sociality into the instruments of exchange, culminating in the absorption of humanity itself into the most developed sectors of the monetary system:

> Credit is the *economic* judgement of the *morality* of a man ... Human individuality, human *morality*, have become both articles of commerce and the *material* which money inhabits. The substance, the body clothing the *spirit of money* is not money, paper, but instead it is my personal existence, my flesh and blood, my social worth and status. Credit no longer actualizes money-values in actual money but in human flesh and human hearts.[8]

Whatever the polemical virtues of this account—and it sounds as true as anything Baudrillard ever said about the simulations of the capitalist code—it remains firmly within Hegelian coordinates. Credit appears as a kind of corrupt Absolute Idea developing itself in ever higher spirals of alienated activity within a hollowed-out community. Although it might seem, Marx argues, that credit would allow for the purest, most transparent (because abstract) form of mutual recognition, it is in fact the most direct form of subjugation, because it takes on the dimensions of a whole social and cultural order. The one who must accept credit (the debtor) submits to the judgment of the creditor, who stands for the judgment of *all those who possess wealth*. Credit becomes a more thorough way to mediate the struggle between master and slave: everyone who participates in the struggle thereby becomes committed to maintaining its formal structure. To put it another way, Marx here understands the credit

8   Karl Marx, "Excerpts from James Mill's *Elements of Political Economy*," in *Early Writings*, ed. Quintin Hoare (New York: Vintage Books, 1975), p. 264.

system as the alienation of an essential social "wealth," and based on that understanding, "debt" appears as the negation of an originary or potential plenitude.

If, on the contrary, debt does not arise as the negation of wealth but rather out of an ineradicable friction between lived existence and the maintenance of a social structure, it must be, strictly speaking, *constitutive of the social body*; because life continues and time passes by, all contingencies must be registered as material conflict. Debt, therefore, comprises every socially articulable expression of the gap between what we have, what we need, and what we want.

This idea becomes clearer in the second, more strictly economic phase of Marx's thinking, where debt is treated as the monetary correlative of bodily needs and the realm of necessity. Here the condition of indebtedness appears as a distinctly historical phenomenon, the result of the creation of "free subjects" after a people's release from feudal obligations and enslavement. Insofar as it registers mutual dependence only as a loss of self-sufficiency, indebtedness subtends all market relations. In the *Grundrisse*, Marx offers a derisory portrait of the capitalist who thinks the worker "owes an obligation to capital for the fact that he is alive at all."[9] In the first volume of *Capital*, the idea that debt is grounded in survival appears several times, most strikingly in a long footnote detailing the ways debtors since ancient Rome were subject to dismemberment as punishment for a failure to pay. It seems that Marx believes in the sacrificial origins of debt, and he is ready to quote *The Merchant of Venice* whenever he wants to emphasize the primordial violence that backs the monetary form of capital. Debtors are archetypal figures whose punishment before the law is attributed figuratively to all workers on the job: like the ancient debtor, every proletarian is said to be "skinned" and "bled" and "tortured."[10]

---

9 Karl Marx, *Grundrisse*, trans. Martin Nicolaus (New York: Vintage Books, 1973), p. 293. Henceforth cited as *Grundrisse*.

10 Karl Marx, *Capital*, Volume 1, trans. Ben Fowkes (New York: Vintage Books, 1977), p. 400.

Throughout the first volume of *Capital*, then, indebtedness is no longer a formal or spiritual position. Instead, indebted bodies are precisely what capital takes for granted on every level. Here is the legacy of originary accumulation, renewed at every turn: indebtedness is the primary "enclosure" of the lived body, the inaugural biopolitical event. They become the working bodies of wage labor, the unemployed bodies of the reserve industrial army, the starving bodies of "unproductive" and "uncompetitive" enterprises, and, everywhere, the bodies whose appetites can only be fed by submitting to the law of debt. In sum, debts are the means by which misery becomes socialized.

While "debt" tends to call forth concrete metaphors of the body, much of what Marx has to say about "credit" in *Capital* relates to the rather abstract, even metaphysical, tendencies of capitalist accumulation and centralization. Here the cluster of connections and distinguishing metaphors is rather different. Credit requires a dispensation from the order of value, grounded in a particular political regime. Credit accompanies the generalization of exchange and property relations, and serves as the means by which these processes are turned into symbolic games in order to expand their domain.[11] Marx emphasizes that credit tends toward an ideal synchronization of value on a national and a global scale: as in the 1844 notes, credit is here understood as a "perfection" of the social functions performed by money, but now this perfection is treated as a real technical accomplishment, the consolidation of a hitherto chaotic process and the mobilization of vast untapped resources of organization and rationalization. In his major work, Marx treats the credit system in a more dynamic dialectical fashion than his earlier judgments allowed: although credit is still seen as the hub of collective blindness and roguish trickery, it deploys and transmits ever vaster and more volatile forces of production. It is this power of control that makes the credit system seem to

11   *Grundrisse*, pp. 495, 659.

be the embodiment of wealth in its most pure form. But Marx came to recognize that the very idea of "wealth" was not the *conceptual basis* but the *ideological alibi* of economic rationality. By defining all social production in terms of abstract wealth, economists construct a system in which capital literally takes credit for everything: all past accomplishments are reckoned as "its" achievements and measured in its coinage, and all future projects are meant to submit to its standards of judgment. It is not the exchange of so-called equivalent values but the obligation to express everything in the form of value that binds together the social project of capitalism.

Although this logic would insist that there cannot be debt without credit and vice versa, there can be no symmetry between the terms. Indeed, in their conjuncture and disjuncture, they constitute a dynamic and unstable antagonism. Under capitalism, and now more than ever, there is credit without debt for the few (who can wield the power of investment without accountability) and debt without credit for the many (who bear the hazards without exercising a choice). Yet the condition of indebtedness will always outlive the necessities and the credits that extract value from it. That is its irreducible and ineradicable secret. If *credit* is understood as the sweeping gesture with which capital lays claim to the present in the name of the past and the future, *debt* may be seen as a mark of the nonsynchronous, the stubborn insistence of everything resistant to economic rule. If creating credit *ex nihilo* is a sublime projection of an economic order and system, indebtedness must be the deferral or withdrawal of value, a way to play for time in order to keep something alive. Can it be said that we owe our lives— our needs and desires, our sense of self and collectivity—to this constantly reenacted withdrawal into indebtedness? Marx insists that we ought to find radical prospects in the most advanced edge of capitalist logic: we can locate that edge in the disposition of indebtedness, which forestalls the hour of necessity and anticipates the moment of freedom.

And so our reading of Marx leads us to pursue a rather unexpected question: does indebtedness, which might once have seemed to be the most inescapable trap of capital, in fact offer us a lever with which to overturn it? Is there a special role for debt in emancipatory thinking? And in order to send this story homeward, I should ask, What does this Marxist understanding of debt have to do with the debts faced by Hans Röckle, the playful magician?

Here we have to turn to the third and final dimension of Marx's views on debt, found in the third volume of *Capital*. There, in the remarkable twenty-seventh chapter, after having bitterly denounced the trickery of haute finance, Marx argues that the credit system, despite *and* because of the bad magic it practices, offers a glimpse of the kind of magic we would need to exercise in order to achieve a realm of collective freedom. It is here that the dialectical tensions elaborated earlier become explosive and therefore hopeful:

> The credit system ... accelerates the material development of the productive forces and the creation of the world market ... At the same time, credit accelerates the violent outbreaks of this contradiction, crises, and with these elements the dissolution of the old mode of production.
>
> The credit system has a dual character immanent in it: on the one hand it develops the driving force of capitalist production, enrichment through the exploitation of others' labor, into the purest and most colossal system of gambling and swindling, and restricts ever more the already small number of the exploiters of social wealth; but on the other hand, it establishes the form of transition to a new mode of production.[12]

It is precisely the so-called fictionality of credit, its ungrounded constitution of a productive collectivity, that serves as both the symbolic condition of and real barrier to the accumulation of capital, but in presenting this immense productivity as a collective

12   Karl Marx, *Capital*, Volume 3, trans. David Fernbach (New York: Vintage Books, 1981), p. 572.

conjuration on the unsecured imaginary plane, the credit system ceaselessly reveals what can be and has been accomplished by the whole system of social labor. As long as capital can tell this story as if itself were the only real agent, the fictionality of that scenario will hide the work of all those who make every story happen. But the story can be told in another way, no more and no less fictitious, in which this unconscious collectivity recognizes its investments in the present, claims the imaginary powers of this system as its own, and thereby makes its wishes known. Faced with the terrifying spectacle of colossal debts, ranging from the most intimate to the most public, we can learn from Marx to look for that which makes them possible: the living acts of collective imagination that might yet find a way to recall and reclaim their own creative powers.

Marx goes no further than this in explaining how the worst thing about capitalism could become the very thing that can undo its strictest bindings. But even if these hints are not enough to tell us what a revolution would look like, they do offer a lesson in reading, which would be the final lesson we can learn from Eleanor's story: No matter how dangerous the world of history may appear, that is where our adventures will always take us. The moment of hope can be glimpsed neither in the debt that inaugurates the story nor in the tale that it obligates each of us to read, but rather it is to be found in the prospect of return, where history is reopened by extinguishing the story that led us there. In trying to imagine ourselves waiting for everything that has been sent away painfully to come back at last, we learn what it would mean to take responsibility for our own promises, to be the recipients of our own gifts, over and over again. Who would we have to be, to believe that such a return is possible? We would have to be, somehow or other, children: not the faithful descendants or the loyal inheritors of Marx, but simply those who look forward to living a good and happy life, and who recognize Marx as one of our own kind.

7 The Dialectic of Indebtedness

Life's given to no man outright; all must borrow.
—Lucretius, *On the Nature of Things*, III, 968

Nothing obligates us to reckon with history, except history. There would be no need to think about history if it always flowed like a river or rolled back and forth like a tide, indifferent to whatever we might have to say about it. And so when we say that history opens possibilities or sets limits, expands horizons or shrinks them, bears promises or poses dangers, delivers surprises or disappoints expectations, we are not simply describing a particular state of things or recording a series of events, but expressing that we are implicated in something much more dynamic and complex. Whether or not it ever takes shape as something else—a story, a structure, a project, or a destiny—history always makes its presence known by drawing us in its movements, even and especially when we come to realize that we were already there. That is why "thinking about history" is an everyday task: it's the way we learn to deal with whatever happens to us, the way we handle it, cope with it, bargain with it. And every day we discover that the way we think about history gets woven into the way things happen, prompting us to think it through all over again. This insistent experience of historicity—the whole friction and torque of daily life in its ordinary and extraordinary moments alike—never feels like a free and equal exchange between our selves and our situation. On the contrary, exactly because it feels stressed and uneven, we tend to treat the experience of historicity through the language of obligation and indebtedness, as we try to figure out what we owe—if anything—to ourselves, to others, to whatever already exists and to what might yet come to be.

Of course, it is always possible to fail, or to refuse, to reckon with history. People do it all the time, whether through stubbornness, defiance, forgetfulness, or sheer impotence. Every effective reckoning with history is also a reckoning with whatever leaves us unbalanced, when the social and psychic debts appear unpaid and unpayable. Giorgio Agamben has described this difficult position in a delicate way: we are always indebted because "humankind's most proper being—being potential—is in a certain sense lacking, insofar as it can not-be." To have "potential," to see ourselves in light of what might be, is not yet an accomplishment and not yet a disappointment. The very act of living opens onto a lack that might not be filled, a debt that might not be fulfilled. That is no reason to hesitate—quite the contrary. We owe it to ourselves to honor every debt that offers us a good chance to live more fully. At the same time, we ought to be able to reject what we owe, repudiating or expropriating any debt that diminishes our potential to live at all. That is the aim of a materialist understanding of history: it undertakes the most meticulous accounting of our efforts to face what faces us, in order to know where to push upon our own potential as well as to locate precise targets for our infidelity to the current order of things. Learning how and why to break obligations can be just as important, and just as difficult, as learning how and why to keep them. The debts that might have seemed obscurely intimate might turn out to be irreducibly collective, and those that seemed essentially universal might be faced only by crystallizing them in absolutely singular ways.

So we live between two debts. On one hand, there is the ineradicable debt described by Agamben that comes from having or being a potentiality that we can never really possess, exhaust, or fulfill, which prompts us to live as if we were always in pursuit of something else, like happiness, which can never be ours alone. On the other hand, there is the full array of as yet unreckoned debts that constitute the complex historical situation in which we live, ranging from unresolved family romances and the duties of identity to the very persistent obligations imposed by the dominant forms of political and economic power. A practical orientation toward the overdetermined complexity of history demands that we learn both to bind and to break our debts, coupling a willful effort to preserve and augment our common powers with a determined refusal to capitulate to the regime of the always already there.

Let me stress this notion of a "practical orientation" toward history. We often name the coordinates of our historical situation through ordinary gestures—combining hand and eye, earth and stars—where the simplest act of pointing in one direction reveals a whole field of other things already in place and exerting their pull.[1] Such gestures inhabit even the broadest abstractions—facticity, historicity, situatedness, worldliness—with which we designate not only what is "there," but also how "what there is" is already organized, exteriorized, even capitalized, in a way that makes life (this life or any life) more or less livable.

The very idea that we live in history as a kind of immediate and infinite indebtedness can be understood as a defining attitude of modernity. On one hand, as Nietzsche described, human societies undergo a ruthlessly inward reorganization as soon as each person internalizes the drama of obligation within himself. Subjectivity twists itself into a perpetually bad conscience, deferring its sovereign powers to a higher order that, in default of anything else, is none other than "value" itself, raised to a moral eminence. The

---

1   The key phrase here is drawn from Jacques Rancière, *The Names of History: On the Poetics of Knowledge*, trans. Hassan Melehy (Minneapolis: University of Minnesota Press, 1994). The emphasis on the naming of history as a kind of "orientation" takes its cue from Alexander Kluge and Oskar Negt, who describe "orientation" as the "Urform of theoretical work" in *Geschichte und Eigensinn*, Band 2, *Der Unterschätzte Mensch* (Frankfurt: Zweitausendeins, 2001), p. 1002.

structural and rhetorical permutations of that defaulted or deferred sovereignty thus constitute so many different apparatuses of indebtedness. On the other hand, as Polanyi describes it, by generalizing value relations throughout the social order, human societies turn inside out, held together by nothing but exchange and the enforcement of exchange. Capitalism is that apparatus of indebtedness in which all debts, public and private, pass through the cash nexus. Postmodernity, as Jameson describes it, would be the moment when this process has run its course, so that the only common element animating the global historical situation is the virtually universal obligation to participate in the world of markets, which have staked a claim upon everything once produced and protected within the framework of more restricted and protective social arrangements. The key historical task at the moment, then, is to find a way to constitute, beyond that impasse, a properly historical connection between indebtedness and the common good on a global scale. Here, in order to trace just the outline of the problem, I want to show how indebtedness is inscribed in three pairs of very familiar and very basic historical concepts. By describing how we are bound up with history—through a series of theoretical orientation exercises—we might find out just how far we're able to deal with it (in all senses of that phrase) differently.

Recall once again the famous passage in *The Eighteenth Brumaire,* where Marx describes the burden of dead generations weighing like a nightmare on the living. "Men make their own history, but not of their own free will; not under circumstances they have themselves chosen but under the given and inherited circumstances with which they are directly confronted."[2]

---

2 Karl Marx, "The Eighteenth Brumaire of Louis Bonaparte," in *Surveys from Exile,* ed. David Fernbach (New York: Vintage, 1974), p. 146. For a reading of comparable formulations in Marx and Engels, emphasizing the conceptual problems with the identity of the "men" who are supposed to make history, see Étienne Balibar, "The Basic Concepts of Historical Materialism," in Louis Althusser and Étienne Balibar, *Reading Capital,* trans. Ben Brewster (London: Verso, 1979), pp. 207–8 and 251–2.

This marvelously recursive sentence has been glossed and paraphrased so many times that one might overlook the exact formulation at its core: "given and inherited circumstances." What might sound like Marx's redundant stuttering seems on reflection to be especially well phrased. Given *and* inherited, what's taken *and* what's received, what remains *and* what is passed along: the phrase opens up several distinct settings in which historical circumstances confront us and are confronted, where the dispositions of agency and determination still remain to be seen. Indeed, Sartre quotes Marx's phrase and remarks, "Dialectical rationality, the whole of which is contained in this sentence, must be seen as the permanent and dialectical unity of freedom and necessity."[3] Yet this unity nowhere presents itself as such: both freedom and necessity become known (if they do) only in passing, as presuppositions or implications. In the meantime people deal with history as a compound mixture of exigencies, obligations, and potentialities that have to be worked through in practice, on their own terms, collectively and immanently. The only real contradictions at stake do not occur between people and their circumstances, but within the modalities of the engagement itself.

Let's slow down and weigh each word. "The given" does not designate what is just there now, but what must have been somehow already there when we got here. It involves more than an inventory of facts or "everything that is the case." Its priority assumes the force of necessity without dictating its vector: "the given" includes whatever has to be taken into account, no matter what we do. There is something unsettling about the given. One does not "confront" a given situation as a subject faces an object, but through a process of give-and-take, in which what is "given" must be both taken up and given back in the very movement by which one finds oneself in its midst. The "givenness" of circumstances, far from being inert, punctual, solid, or assured, must be drawn out through our encounter with it,

---

3 Jean-Paul Sartre, *Critique of Dialectical Reason*, trans. Alan Sheridan-Smith (London: Verso, 1976), p. 35.

and that always takes time: it is only in the course of that encounter that the materiality of the world comes to matter to us. The intricate ramifications of these words have been traced by Heidegger, and Derrida after him, starting from the etymologies of "gift" [*es gibt, ça donne*]. In speaking of the "given" world as something already there, we treat it *as a gift*—as something that does not finally command us because it leaves open the possibility of our response—because in the act of acceptance we both appropriate the gift and forget how it got there.[4] In that doubled movement of appropriation and forgetting, we reenact, on our own behalf, the gift that bestows existence. This constantly reiterated reenactment of giving is not a mere reflex of psychic life: it takes a material form, as something supplementary and prosthetic, in particular as gesture and speech, which serve as fundamental techniques of anticipation and articulation. Human beings become capable of doing whatever they do, for better or worse, only by giving themselves to themselves "technically," by means of the given. (This would be Bernard Stiegler's more contemporary way of understanding Heidegger's proposition that Dasein " 'historizes' out of its future on each occasion."[5])

Yet it is not the giving but the taking-up that opens the future orientation of historicity. If, on one hand, the notion of "given circumstances" marks an irreducibly existential and phenomenological dimension of materiality, the phrase "inherited circumstances" [*überlieferten Umständen*] indicates a different dimension, a distinctly social and collective one. Indeed, it is telling that Heidegger argued the need for an analysis of the "given" precisely because the "inherited," as an untrustworthy and contentious tradition, so easily conditions us to accept its already established meanings. In Marx,

---

4 Jacques Derrida, *Given Time: I. Counterfeit Money*, trans. Peggy Kamuf (Chicago: University of Chicago Press, 1992), pp. 23–4.

5 See Bernard Stiegler, *Technics and Time, I: The Fault of Epimetheus*, trans. Richard Beardsworth and George Collins (Palo Alto: Stanford University Press, 1998), especially pp. 204–16. The quoted phrase comes from Martin Heidegger, *Sein und Zeit* (Tübingen: Max Niemeyer Verlag, 1993), p. 20.

however, each term draws out something essential that the other does not say. The idea that we *inherit* our circumstances necessarily reminds us that they have been made by others and passed along, but also that inheritance makes a demand upon us, that we have to make ourselves the heirs of what has gone before. For all of its legal trappings and aura of piety, the process is fraught with inequalities and injustice. You have to fight over inheritances, whether you win or lose over the other claimants; by the same token, it cannot be certain that we always accept an inheritance, and even when we do, that our "acceptance" will be anything like a genuine choice or a faithful continuity. (As Derrida puts it in *Spectres of Marx*, "Inheritance is never a *given*, it is always a task."[6]) We also cannot be certain that everything bequeathed by the dead generations will arrive; just the opposite, materialists will always wonder about everything lost in transit or disfigured by the passage. Even more important than the path of any particular inheritance is what Bourdieu might call the durable disposition to inherit, the persistent need to stitch what we are about to do back to what has been done before. Although the disposition to inherit secures the persistence of every kind of group lineage, it can be "the source of misadaptation as well as adaptation, revolt as well as resignation" in such a way that any of those outcomes, far from stopping the lineage, will be added to the inheritance as well.[7] The *Eighteenth Brumaire*, of course, emphasizes the tricks of misrecognition, wrapped up in anxiety and guilt, that accompany crucial acts of historical inheritance. Recall that Marx offers his fundamental propositions about history-making as a preface to his polemical description of "world-historical necromancy," in which bourgeois revolutionaries draped themselves in the glories of the past because they could not face the fact that they were "engaged

---

6   Jacques Derrida, *Spectres of Marx*, trans. Peggy Kamuf (New York: Routledge, 1994), p. 54.

7   Pierre Bourdieu, *The Logic of Practice*, trans. Richard Nice (Palo Alto: Stanford University Press, 1990), p. 62.

in the revolutionary transformation of themselves and their material surroundings." People make their own history, then, not by willfully transcending the given or forswearing all inheritance, but by trying to take those pressures, no matter how weighty or obscure, upon themselves.

But perhaps the time when people could readily imagine themselves as the subjects of their own history in such terms is long past, not least because the circumstances we confront directly hardly ever seem like the most decisive ones. The lived dimension of needs has been absorbed, reinvented, and recalibrated by the advanced operations of commodification, so that the concept of necessity itself seems ever more fungible and yet more absolute at the same time. By the same token, the very idea of "inheriting" the dead labor of previous generations is as likely to seem a curse as a blessing, precisely because its cumulative weight imposes so many unavoidable obligations. There are too many mistaken accomplishments, too much unfinished business, too many unpaid bills. Perhaps, before Marx, the "given and inherited" might once have referred, relatively unproblematically, to something like the distinction between nature and culture, to immediate materiality on one hand and the palpable survival of the ancien régime on the other. By naming these antecedents in this way, Marx draws a line under them: henceforth they become stakes for open political contestation. From this perspective, the task of making history would always have to be pursued as if we were restaging the inaugural act of modernity, breaking the spell of the merely existent and upsetting the laws of the already settled in order to bring forth something new. But in learning how to trace the exercise of such freedom, people also learn just how attached to circumstances they have to be: every historical act begins and ends bound up in debt.

Indebtedness need not be fatal. If a society could actually ensure the inheritance of its own accomplishments on behalf of those who created them, and for the sake of those who need them most, such a continuity might really deserve to be called progress. That every society actually fails to do so, and hides its failure in forgetful neglect and well-fortified forms of needless privilege, is a perpetual disaster. At least that is how one might understand the sense of this blunt note in Benjamin's *Passagen-Werk*:

> The concept of progress should be based on the idea of catastrophe. That things "just keep on going" *is* the catastrophe. It is not what always awaits, but what is always given.[8]

If the twentieth century ever gets its headstone, this note could be its epitaph. Indeed its tones—more famously rendered in the fragment on Klee's *Angelus Novus*—resonate throughout many critiques of modernity. Its key terms were carried over in restatements by Arendt and Adorno, but the thrust of Benjamin's remark could just as well have been taken up by a range of others, from Bataille and Blanchot to Debord and Bookchin. ("Armageddon has been in effect—go get a late pass," said Public Enemy in 1988.) Taken as an expression of everyday experience, Benjamin's key phrase ("That things 'just keep on going' *is* the catastrophe") describes a potent mixture of ongoing drudgery and recurrent disappointment, when every pious reference to the achievements of the past or to the possibilities of the future tastes like death warmed over. Taken as a summary unmasking of "progress" and "development"—for decades the ideological carrier waves that sustained the reproduction of social relations and that even now are being polished off for a new round of restructurings—the sentence still has its bite. At the same time, it has a frankness that offers no relief: it reminds us of something we try not to acknowledge except with a bitter laugh. Every great transformation of the world has brought about a systematic expansion of suffering. We might as well reverse the saying: the doctrine of progress

---

8   Walter Benjamin, *Das Passagen-Werk* (Frankfurt: Suhrkamp Verlag, 1982), p. 592. The note is numbered [N9a, 1].

has become so catastrophic that even the idea of catastrophe has progressed. Although progress has lost much of its positive content and public usefulness, the concept of catastrophe has been able to take over, and in a perfect ruse of reason has become the stick that waves in front of our eyes where the carrot used to be. Once upon a time, progress could justify any catastrophe; now it is catastrophe that justifies everything, whether we call it progress or not.

So we would miss Benjamin's point if we thought that catastrophe was the "truth" of progress, or its end. The two concepts have to be thought together, even if any attempt to draw up a balance sheet between them immediately becomes grotesque. When we turn to official statistics or development reports, all genuine concepts of history fall silent, pushed to the top and the bottom of each chart, framing from the outside the awful legibility of every quantitative comparison and distinction. As we have seen already, much of the official discourse on "what is" amounts to a reiteration of the simple fact that the rich really do keep getting richer, and the poor really do die sooner. If, as Adorno said, the possibility of progress has migrated to the global subject of "humanity," surely catastrophe has followed the same path; but such global subjects suffer both their globality and their subjectivity in the form of helplessness.[9] It is pointless to hope for progress without disaster precisely because catastrophe has always been the internalized condition—and the externalized cost— for whatever claimed to be progress. How many generations, thinking themselves already modern, have already lived and died waiting for progress finally to break clear of catastrophe, when that was never part of the program?

At the level of everyday life, the achieved unity of progress and catastrophe can be seen in the logic of *killing time*, which may be late capitalism's most advanced contribution to the repertoire of human spirit. It is constantly reinvented in new cultural forms (for example,

9   Theodor Adorno, *Critical Models*, trans. Henry W. Pickford (New York: Columbia University Press, 1998), p. 144.

in the fusion of traffic jams and mobile phones) and now finds new life in the latest economic projects. This logic might be described as "preemptive development," as it generates hypertrophied sprawl without inhabitants, promiscuous growth without infrastructure. "Killing time" does not mean standing still or doing nothing. It means *taking up time* precisely by *taking up space*. This mutation is decisive. For example, in their book *Great Leap Forward*, the Harvard Design School's Project on the City has described a twenty-first-century Chinese variant, spotted in the immense sprawl of the Pearl River delta. They quote an extravagantly boosterish description of a brand-new metropolis: "Zhuhai city, with beautiful scenery and good environment, HAS BECOMING a famous scenic spot for tourism and a garden for investment, it is the result of Zhuhai people's wisdom and courage." In a cheeky twist, the Harvard group declared that this awkward verb phrase ("has becoming") offers the best description of the paradoxical temporality driving the sudden and comprehensive development of southern China. Its industrialization and urbanization is already done but still under way, combining "the immediacy of achievement with eternal deferment." This is not open-ended development but the fastest route into a dead end, in other words, "*terminal striving.*"[10] Advancing very rapidly or not at all, the inertial forces of backfill modernization produce massive if unfinished facts on the ground: runaway cities whose collapse would be worse than their expansion, chicken-fight industrial strategies, and race-to-the-bottom welfare schemes, all tied into webs of dependency and vulnerability that cannot be cut apart without risking general ruin. Every truly lasting historical process may turn out to be, as the current keyword says, ultimately unsustainable, and capitalism is exactly what occupies the meantime.

Yet that bleak prognosis cannot be the last word, even for Benjamin. In his notes on the philosophy of history, Benjamin repeatedly

10   Harvard Design School Project on the City, *Great Leap Forward*, ed. Chuihua Judy Chung, Jeffrey Inaba, Rem Koolhaas, Sze Tsung Leong (Köln: Taschen, 2001), p. 706.

opposes the spectacle of progress and catastrophe to the aporetic thought that the history of the oppressed is marked by discontinuity. Whereas the history of the oppressors conveys the continuity of obligations, embodied in material things and historical concepts, the tradition of the oppressed teaches the strategy of interruption and disconnection, the moment of flashing up and breaking apart. In such a moment, all bets are off and all debts are cancelled. As the first moments of the Paris Commune showed, redemption might arrive not when the revolutionary messiah appears but when the pawn shops are closed and the back rents are cancelled. But by the same token, no matter how much upheaval may be unleashed, such events can never simply start over at zero. There is something positively schizo about the *Jetztzeit*: it could happen at any time, but it doesn't happen until it happens, and even then it doesn't just happen. Benjamin knows this complexity inside out, and his texts offer fitful explorations of that complex interval between wishful expectation and dread, teaching us to practice different modalities of anticipation and suspension, long patience and outright refusal. A clue about these conflicted moods can be found in one of his late notes, meditating on a poem by Brecht:

> [line scratched out:] Example of genuine historical representation: 'An die Nachgeborenen.' We claim from those born later not thanks for our victories but rather remembrance for our defeats. [not scratched out:] That is consolation: the only kind that can be given to those who have no more hope for consolation.[11]

If indeed "the enemy has not ceased to be victorious," it need not be a declaration of surrender to say so.

To claim remembrance for what we could not do may seem like the smallest favor with which to trouble future generations, but it

---

11   Walter Benjamin, *Gesammelte Schriften*, Band I/iii (Frankfurt: Suhrkamp Verlag), p. 1,240.

may be too much to ask nevertheless. Our consolation ought not to matter to them, if they have accomplished what we could not. And if they, too, have been defeated, our acknowledgment of defeat should not provide any consolation to them, either.

Indeed, Brecht's famous poem explains that the discontinuities of history are not always advantageous. To feel out of sync with the times, to be unable to do what ought to have been simple, to treat almost everything in life as a personal achievement or an intimate threat even though almost none of it is: all of this keeps us from living in any of the ways we might otherwise be able to do.

Benjamin speaks of "our defeats," Brecht speaks of "our weaknesses," and they are talking about the same history, if not exactly the same thing. Of course, the literature of Marxism is full of meditations on failure and defeat. The distinction between these two terms serves as a basic compass for political judgment, always complicated by the way victories are reversed and undone. In the whole tradition, Sartre's *Critique* provides the most thorough compendium of examples of how, at every scale of historical process—from factory work to the consolidation of revolutionary movements—events implacably turn against their subjects. As soon as the problem is posed this way, it becomes startlingly clear that the longest-lasting strands of Marxist discourse are those grounded in defeat, hinging on the experience of one reversal after another. It is not necessary to go through every example to see how this distinction structures drastically different narratives and strategies. (We know the Paris Commune was a defeat, but what about Nicaragua? We could say that the antiwar movement did not stop the war in Iraq, but is it a failure?) At best, the judgment of defeat leads back to a more thorough analysis of the victor's—the enemy's—strengths, while the judgment of failure turns toward a corrective and therapeutic diagnosis of one's own weaknesses. Yet there is no reason to make such judgments except to call into being a collectivity capable of establishing their truth. As opposed to the more coolly conceptual notions of dominance and hegemony, the notions of defeat and failure never lose their unsettling sting, which is why they, rather than some idea of ultimate success, mark the place of the Real in revolutionary discourse.

That is how we can approach, on one hand, the statement made by Perry Anderson when he relaunched the *New Left Review* in January 2000:

> The only starting-point for a realistic Left today is a lucid registration of historical defeat . . . No collective agency able to match the power of capital is yet on the horizon . . . But if the human energies for a change of system are ever released again, it will be from within the metabolism of capital itself. We cannot turn away from it. Only in the evolution of this order could lie the secrets of another one.[12]

And alongside it, this remark by Fredric Jameson:

> [The] vocation of Utopia lies in failure . . . its epistemological value lies in the walls it allows us to feel around our minds, the invisible limits it gives us to detect by sheerest induction, the miring of our imaginations in the mode of production itself, the mud of the present age in which the winged Utopian shoes stick, imagining that to be the force of gravity itself.[13]

There is something breathtaking about both of these statements. They are hard to take. I don't think either position has anything to do with what is usually called optimism or pessimism; just the opposite, each one lays down a challenge to imagine how the harshest historical judgments can nevertheless be *enabling*. I could press the point by saying—and I'm not the first to do so—that the only

12   Perry Anderson, "Renewals," New *Left Review* 1 (Second Series) January/February 2000, pp. 16–7.
13   Fredric Jameson, *Seeds of Time* (New York: Columbia University Press, 1994), p. 75.

real leverage against the present conjuncture that Marxist thinking offers concerns its ability to *declare defeat* and to *recognize failure* in a way that puts every kind of accomplishment and aspiration in question. But to see the present moment as defeat *and* failure *at the same time* requires a paradoxical conjugation of repudiation and fidelity. One must be able to go through defeat *without saving anything*, and to go through failure *without losing everything*, but there is no way to know in advance what will be given up and what will be kept. To declare an epochal defeat and, at the same time, to pronounce yet another failure looks like a terribly risky political strategy, endangering both our critical faculties and our Utopian wishes. But the alternative should be plain enough to see: to exclude such words from our vocabulary would leave us nothing to do but jostle for a better place in that triumphal procession already underway.

Indeed, all of the names of history must be invoked against the vision of a victorious capitalism that declares itself (along with its most powerful states) the sole bearer of human accomplishment. As I've tried to suggest, each name bears its own kind of historicity, its own inflections and limits marked by the moments of its ongoing articulation. In that sense the lexicon we have been tracing outlines a rough evolutionary scheme, each word knotted with another, each knot serving as a contingent figure of historical indebtedness, the whole line drawing tighter each time: first, we have the fundamental thinking of historical being, in terms of existential and ontological implication, entwined with socially binding obligations; second, the appearance in modernity of a collective horizon of expectation, interwoven with disappointment and destruction; and third, in an era where necessity is universally expressed as a relationship of capital, the encounter with one's historical circumstances, which finds its most decisive expression in what is refused and unrealized.

All of these names remain *on this side* of the future: they demarcate the different dimensions of indebtedness that compose our common experience of history. Everywhere we turn we find the force of the given and the inherited, progress and catastrophe, defeat and failure—all transformed by the spectacle of contemporary capitalism into infinite indebtedness. In the face of such debts we keep learning the same vital lesson: the only way to bear the dead weight of history is to push back against it.

Conclusion: Who's Afraid of Jubilee?

In 2008, when Iceland's banking system collapsed after years of aggressive expansion, popular protests drove out the country's ruling party. When Latvia's housing bubble burst and its hot flows of credit dried up, its economy went from being the fastest-growing in Europe to the fastest-shrinking, and a newly elected government was urged to slash its budget and "euroize" its currency. As their situations worsened, both Iceland and Latvia began to resemble Argentina in 2001, when its economy crashed and public pressure expelled several governments in quick succession. But there turned out to be a big difference: whereas Argentina spurned IMF prescriptions and tried to rescue itself, the center-left governments in Iceland and Latvia accepted the supervision of the IMF, hoping not only that a quick infusion of money would restart their economies, but also that fiscal discipline would restore their access to the world credit markets. More recently, the excruciating, months-long dance of the European governments around the bailout of Greece hinged on a similar issue: who would dictate terms for the surrender of what remained of the Greek economy—the European Central Bank, the IMF, the German chancellor, the bond rating agencies, or everybody all at once? In any case, it would be the riot police who were (and still are) expected to convince the population that there can be no appeal against the new fiscal regime.

It is one thing to appease bankers and bond traders, but something else to appease restive populations—as Dennis C. Blair, then

Obama's director of national intelligence, recognized in 2009 when he declared that global economic turmoil now posed the greatest threat to the US and other governments around the world. His comments echoed earlier warnings from Treasury Secretary Henry Paulson and IMF chief Dominique Strauss-Kahn, both of whom predicted there would be civil unrest unless their rescue plans were followed.[1] Of course, they should have also predicted that there would be riots precisely because of the rescue plans. Whether it is a question of ballooning government deficits or austerity plans, disappearing pensions, lost jobs and homes, or a thousand other factors leading to shrunken life possibilities, there is no telling how much debt people can bear. A new politics of indebtedness is emerging everywhere—in government ministries and parliaments, workplaces and households, streets and forests. Its alternatives run the gamut from deferral, negotiation, and capitulation all the way to confrontation, evasion, and outright refusal. What follows is a tentative outline of the possibilities and outer limits of this new politics.

In the almost always vexed relationship between international banks and sovereign governments, there is no infallible blueprint for dealing with crippling debts. Nigeria, flush with oil money, eagerly paid off the bulk of its external debts, but Ecuador chose to default on its bonds, despite having the money to make payments, because its government considered the obligations not only onerous but illegally imposed. Across Africa, longstanding debts to the West are being retired or cancelled, even as China spreads a new wave of loans and grants. In Asia, governments who felt burned by the 1997 financial crisis have built up a firewall of regulations and currency reserves to avoid the need for Western-style rescues. In contrast to the decades when "Third World debt" gripped virtually

---

1   Mark Mazzetti, "Global Economic Crisis Poses Top Threat to U.S., Spy Chief Warns," *New York Times*, February 13, 2009, p. A14. For Paulson and Strauss-Kahn's remarks, and for an excellent description of the situation in Iceland, see Rebecca Solnit, "The Icelandic Volcano Erupts," available online: tomdispatch.com

the entire global south, the picture today is much more varied and, compared to the old images of the "debt trap" and "debt bomb," somewhat harder to read. It is worth recalling Eric Hobsbawm's assessment of the early 1980s debt crisis: "probably the most dangerous moment for the capitalist world economy since 1929."[2] Perhaps we should wonder whether that historical judgment would still hold true, in spite of the events of 2008: after all, what was the collapse of Lehman Brothers, a temporary haircut for the hedge funds, or the evisceration of the "shadow banking system," compared to the near-bankruptcy of Mexico, Argentina, and Brazil?

In a longer perspective, we would need to compare the current sovereign debt crises to earlier moments of default. The nineteenth century saw waves of debt repudiation, nosedive devaluations, and outright bankruptcy, as debts undertaken to jumpstart modernization often proved too demanding to sustain. Revolutions and invasions provided other occasions (some more happy than others) for repudiations and cancellations. Seen from the perspective of creditors, such instances demonstrate the ultimately transient aspect of financial obligations; seen from the point of view of debtors, the historical sequence displays an implacable tightening, as large-scale private and public debts come to be increasingly embedded within a complex global structure backed by political and military force.[3]

But all of that remains within the framework of national jurisdictions and the international financial system. For individuals and localized groups, options in the face of overwhelming indebtedness appear rather fraught at best. In countries where an individual credit

2 Eric Hobsbawm, *The Age of Extremes: A History of the World, 1914–1991* (New York: Vintage Books, 1994), p. 423.

3 See Elmar Altvater, "Historical Debt Cycles," in *The Future of the Market* (London: Verso Books, 1993), pp. 125–78. For a more mainstream discussion of debt cycles—aiming to compare debt crises across a wide variety of historical circumstances—see Carmen M. Reinhart and Kenneth S. Rogoff, "This Time Is Different: A Panoramic View of Eight Centuries of Financial Crises," April, 2008, available online: economics .harvard.edu.

score is becoming the most precious and most vulnerable proof of identity, it is getting easier to go broke but harder to declare bankruptcy. In the United States one often hears stories of defaulted homeowners who simply put the keys in the mailbox and walked away. No doubt there is an element of wishful thinking here: the purgatory of living without credit seems idyllic compared to the hell of living with bad debts. At the furthest extreme, farmers in India, facing both the old village moneylender system and the new pressures of liberalization, have been committing suicide in enormous numbers. But as soon as people recognize that they share their predicament with others, they take more drastic measures. For decades there have been "IMF riots" all around the world, wherever people chafe against the draconian cuts in social provision, privatization schemes, and currency devaluations dictated by orthodox doctrine. Farmers and small business interests in Mexico formed a debtors' union, El Barzón, to pressure the government to change the terms of burdensome debts. Recent events in Spain and Turkey suggest that there is a new kind of flash point, the "pre–IMF riot," where people mobilize against even the prospect of a visit from IMF advisors.

The question "how much debt is too much?" is usually answered in technical terms: when the cost of servicing the debt is greater than the value produced by the debt, something has got to give. In practice, however, there seem to be countless exceptions, debts that persist long after they should have collapsed. Is it possible to designate a consistent tipping point where debt must turn into an impossible burden? Why should there be such a tipping point? Is it possible instead that the limits of indebtedness are no longer, or never were, subject to strictly economic calculation? As the most developed societies face widespread distress from the ongoing crisis, a low-tide mark of public expectations is becoming visible—whether in the form of demands for public provision or for sustained private consumption—that will require the ongoing expansion of debt, come what may. Although it is often expressed in heedless and selfish terms, this kind of intransigent indebtedness might prove to be a genuinely radical position: every attempt to disparage such demands as fiscally irresponsible will have to include an explanation of who really benefits from austerity. And when it turns out that none of the austerity plans on offer do anything more than reinforce the basic imbalances of the prevailing growth regime, electorates may set their governments a new political task: to break the resistance of the creditors, clip the wings of capital flight, recast the terms by which accumulated wealth can be appropriated by the general economy that produced it, and thereby, at last, help the rentier class toward its long-delayed euthanasia.

That is to say, perhaps indebtedness can be a kind of revolt in itself, capable of filling the prevailing order with unrealized demands until it reaches a breaking point. What was the expansion of household debt, including consumer debt and subprime mortgages, but an attempt by a vast swathe of people to lay claim to their financial heaven here on earth? As long as home ownership and the stockpiling of consumer goods are the only available means of seeking a better life, more and more people around the world will surely aim for them. It is important to distinguish the gaudy trappings of consumerism from the political unconscious that drives it. It would be altogether too one-sided to consider the explosion in credit cards, house-flipping, and no-money-down mortgages strictly in terms of the trickery of the creditors: there is no end of that, but what has been revealed in the latest expansion of indebtedness is something much more ambivalent. Think of the example often cited by Thomas Friedman: the California farmworker earning $14,000 a year who acquired a mortgage for a house worth $720,000. Instead of sniffing, as Friedman does, that such people should not be living in such houses, we should ask, "Why not?" In the absence of any comprehensive housing policy, and in light of the manifest inequalities traversed by the circuits of credit, why is the farmworker's leverage any more outrageous than the deals struck on Wall Street every day? Instead of trying to regain some prudent sense of proportion that once again excludes the wrong sort of people from borrowing, shouldn't we aim for a future in which nobody is, as Deleuze put it, "too poor for debt"?

It is not a matter of expanding the areas of social life ruled by debt—that has already happened and there is no going back. It is instead a matter of recognizing how such debts, taken together, express unmet social needs that can be recast as political demands. Surely housing, health care, and education—all of which require expenditures beyond what individuals can pay on their own—should be understood as obligations that everyone owes to anyone, too important to be delegated to the calculations of a financial system indifferent to the common good. And what are pension plans, public and private, but collective attempts to provide for a life without work? All the warnings that pension systems will "run out of money" before fulfilling their mandates typically evade any discussion of the steps necessary to guarantee that the money will be there when it is needed. Everybody knows that there are gargantuan "unfunded liabilities" haunting private and public budgets, so there will have to be a battle of political wills between those who want to find the necessary funds and those who want to reduce the liabilities. So far, the latter camp is winning. We are expected to give up, one by one, all of the socially funded welfare schemes that promised a better life, and instead concede all decisions about what is collectively possible to the accountants. Nevertheless it remains possible to conceive of a genuinely radical counterattack on the terrain of financial reregulation. Can the credit system, instead of accelerating inequality and the false choices of consumerism, serve as a kind of public utility or, better, an institution of collective self-reliance?[4] We would have to

4   This is the question posed by Peter Gowan in his essay "Crisis in the Heartland: Consequences of the New Wall Street System," *New Left Review* 55 (January/February 2009), and by Robin Blackburn in a series of books and essays, including *Banking on Death or, Investing in Life: The History and Future of Pensions* (London: Verso, 2002), especially pp. 465–528, and, more recently, "Value Theory and the Chinese Worker: A reply to Geoff Mann," *New Left Review* 56 (March/April 2009).

invert the statement by Mohammed Yunus, founder of the Grameen Bank, "credit is a basic human right," and say instead, "indebtedness is a basic human condition."

Indeed, microcredit offers a useful example of the attractions and limitations of this line of thinking. By extending loans through local circuits, especially among women, microcredit organizations hope to jumpstart individual initiative and lift poor households out of the worst kinds of poverty. Several models have evolved, from profit-driven branches of established banks to NGO nonprofits and self-organized village credit circles. The basic idea has spread rapidly, especially in South Asia, where there are several millions of borrowers; there are also institutions throughout Africa and South America, but growth on those continents has been slower and more uneven. Viewed at the level of individuals, it is clear that such programs can bring tangible improvements in daily life, in particular for those earning a dollar or two a day. It is also clear that microfinance can lock borrowers into even more inflexible arrangements, reinforced by pressure from fellow borrowers to repay the loans. Given the large claims made on behalf of microcredit schemes—that they spark national development, empower women, and foster more sustainable economies—it is startling to hear, as Connie Bruck reports, that "loans to the poor have not yet had a demonstrable effect on aggregate poverty levels."[5] Likewise Jeremy Seabrook argues that "[it] is asking too much to expect loans for self-employment to overcome structural poverty, and unrealistic to expect it to have any effect at all on growing global inequality." There is no reason to scorn ameliorative measures, unless they block transformative possibilities. The question remains, in Seabrook's words, whether "indebtedness

---

5   Connie Bruck, "Millions for Millions," *The New Yorker*, October 30, 2006, pp. 6–73. Bruck highlights the work of the Grameen Bank in Bangladesh and the Pro Mujer group in Bolivia. For a critical account of microcredit in Bolivia, see "Disobedience Is Happiness: The Art of Mujeres Creando," in *We Are Everywhere*, ed. Notes from Nowhere (London: Verso Books, 2003) pp 256–61.

was ever an agent of liberation."[6] If by "indebtedness" we mean only subjective orientation toward the financial system, the answer must be no.

But there is evidently an exorbitant demand, even a Utopian impulse, built into the concept of microcredit that the current models only begin to approach. By defining success as the social empowerment of women rather than incremental income growth, by doing away with collateral requirements, by plowing interest payments back into the communal fund, some microcredit enterprises break sharply from the mainstream banking model. Where lending services are combined with other social provisions—not only education and health care but also shared technology and local planning—microcredit becomes an instrument of self-organization rather than the cutting edge of capital. At the limit, the question now becomes: can microcredit schemes be designed as self-deconstructing countereconomic processes, undoing the determining power of money in favor of mutually enabled productivity? Rather than functioning as the contagion of financialization spreading into hitherto untouched layers of social life, microcredit could be conceived as the antidote to all of that, the immanent reorganization of indebtedness, capable of repoliticizing precisely those dimensions of social life that have been colonized by market logic.

Nevertheless, it appears that microcredit cannot be scaled upward very far without requiring all kinds of institutional scaffolding—precisely the kind of contraptions that socialists have been trying to design for decades, such as democratic investment boards, differentiated forms of currency, fluid forms of public ownership, and so on. In moving toward such schemes, the idea of a socially shared indebtedness loses something that microcredit has always promised: a chance to recover a more grounded, more accountable kind of economy, subtracted from capitalism. The fact that newer

---

6   Jeremy Seabrook, *The No-Nonsense Guide to World Poverty*, second edition (Oxford: New Internationalist, 2007), p. 129.

microcredit programs have not developed in that direction suggests that this particular kind of indebtedness can thrive only at the more archaic level of the precapitalist market described by Braudel (and discussed in Chapter 1), if not at the level of everyday life itself, where it can save people from destitution only as long as they do not expect to change the overarching conditions that continue to impoverish them.

So it may be too difficult to talk ourselves into this particular Utopian vision. It might seem too much like the ill it seeks to cure, a homeopathic remedy that turns toxic. Instead of tethering the principle of hope to any system of constraints, it might appear more courageous to wish for the abolition of debts altogether, along with the mind-forged manacles that support them. The total cancellation of debts—especially when it points toward the end of the rule of money—certainly seems like the most outlandish Utopian dream imaginable. In fact, this vision has a long history, known in the Judeo-Christian world under the name of Jubilee. As articulated in the twenty-fifth book of Leviticus, a Jubilee should be declared every fifty years, calling for a forgiveness of all debts, the restoration of land and a "redeeming" of houses to their original owners, the freeing of slaves and bond servants, and a suspension of work for the year. In the New Testament, the Jubilee heralds the good news of the fulfillment of the prophecy of Isaiah, revealed at the moment when Jesus announces he will "preach the gospel to the poor," to "heal the brokenhearted, to preach deliverance to the captives, and recovering sight to the blind, to set at liberty them that are bruised" (Luke 4:18). This is not the place to examine why this religious tradition carries along within itself a vision of this undoing and restoration of historical time. Although the idea of Jubilee draws upon religious rhetorics, its vision of liberation remains immediately practical and worldly.

For our purposes here, it is enough to recall that Jubilee keeps returning to inspire revolutionary political movements. As Peter Linebaugh and Marcus Rediker have shown brilliantly, the idea of

Jubilee served as a fundamental touchstone for seventeenth-century English radicals and the eighteenth-century Atlantic working class. It provided a readily available language for a range of antinomian positions, from the most cryptically allegorical to the most literal and secular. (A phrase from Leviticus is imprinted on the Liberty Bell.) As it was crystallized and circulated by the Jamaican Robert Wedderburn, son of an enslaved woman and a slave master, the notion of Jubilee led "in one direction to the general strike and Chartist land policy of the 1830s and in another direction to the abolition of slavery in America."[7] For Linebaugh and Rediker, Jubilee poses an indispensable radical demand, capable of drawing together an unanticipated chain of resistances to capitalist modernity. Linebaugh's more recent book, *The Magna Carta Manifesto*, offers the same lesson drawn from a rather different lineage, aligning relief from debt and the sharing of wealth with the recovery of the commons.

And yet even this Utopian possibility can be compromised, as when religious campaigners and neoliberal policy hawks struck a deal (over the heads of more militant demands) in the wake of the Jubilee 2000 campaign. As we saw in the discussion of Bono and the Gleneagles conference, debts were indeed cancelled, but only to those countries that had already undergone the rigors of economic and political restructuring programs. The most immediate result of the campaign has been to prod countries to follow the prescriptions of the multilateral experts, and to diminish the political standing of those that do not. That explains why so few countries are actually eligible: some are deemed too far gone and others "already recovering." Meanwhile, personal bankruptcy laws are being tightened

---

7   Peter Linebaugh and Marcus Rediker, *The Many-Headed Hydra: Sailors, Slaves, Commoners, and the Hidden History of the Revolutionary Atlantic* (Boston: Beacon Press, 2000), p. 291. The Midnight Notes collective (which includes Linebaugh, Silvia Federici, and George Caffentzis) have also pioneered an antinomian critique of the current debt economy. See their publications (especially Issue 10, "The New Enclosures"), available online: midnightnotes.org.

everywhere, even as the need for borrowing to ride out the downturn increases. It should have been clear all along that the cancellation of debts can actually reinforce the rule of the creditors. In the days of billion-dollar bailouts and backstops, debt relief has become a more urgent issue for bankers than for activists, amid much contrite talk of turning corners and starting over.

Yet the desire to throw off all obligations will continue to generate potent opposition to the current regime of indebtedness. To examine one version of this desire, let us take the example of a well-known radical pamphlet, *The Coming Insurrection*, along with some texts by the French group Tiqqun that stand behind it.[8] The pamphlet devotes most of its space to a withering attack on the prevailing order of things (which they call Empire), followed by a four-part proposal for making an insurrection: first, seize upon the stirrings of refusal; second, cancel social bonds and compose "communes" with other resisters; third, develop self-organization in all its facets; and finally, carry out an insurrection by multiplying and intensifying all of the previous steps. Each of these moments faces its own perils, beginning with the first. How can discontent be turned into revolt? Although many people feel impatience and disillusionment with the world as it is, only those who bypass hesitations or distractions will try to break away from it entirely. The moment of rupture brings the realization that "we must choose sides" (TCI, p. 96). In order to choose sides, one must realize that there are sides to choose: Tiqqun argues that "there are in this society only two parties: the party of those who pretend there is only a single party, and the party of those who know that there are in truth two. Already from this observation, one will know how to recognize ours" (T1, p. 51). In

---

8 The Invisible Committee, *The Coming Insurrection* [trans. unknown] (Los Angeles: Semiotext[e], 2009), henceforth cited in the text as TCI; *Tiqqun: Exercices de Métaphysique Critique*, [Volume 1] (Paris, 1999) and *Tiqqun: Zone d'Opacité Offensive* [Volume 2] (Paris, 2001), henceforth cited as T1 and T2. Much of the Tiqqun material is being republished by La fabrique éditions (lafabrique.fr).

The Coming Insurrection, more bluntly, we hear about "those who want order and those who do not" (p. 12). This way of drawing the battle lines can make strategic sense only if it is acknowledged that there must be some kind of order, a zero degree of staying power, built into the rebellious commune. But the text has a hard time saying that. Instead, the coming together of the commune (in the second moment) is expressed in the most tentative terms: it unfolds through "the promise of the encounter." The decision to form a bond with others comes upon us out of the vicissitudes of the moment, like the swerving atoms in Lucretius coming together to form a new body. But how can it last? Perhaps that is not the right question. The text takes pains to change the terms in which a political body is formed. Thus the promise that binds the communal group is not given by individuals or singularities, but only by the encounter itself. Out of the situation comes a configuration of singularities capable of changing everything. The problem of this promise is really a problem of persistence and consistency: what kind of bond will hold long enough, not only for the potentials of the encounter to be realized, but for fundamental social changes to be brought about?

The book's pervasive suspicion of organization, obedience, identity, and belonging in general poses a dilemma: as long as the authors are denouncing what actually exists, there is no shortage of good targets, especially unions, political parties, governments, and even radical scenes and milieus. But paradoxically enough, it is just when the book begins to talk about "self-defense" that the problem of persistence and consistency becomes urgent. Who or what is being defended? Nothing like a social bond in any of its current acceptations. In *Tiqqun* we can read: "Everything social has become strange to us. We consider ourselves to be absolutely unbound by all *social* obligation, prerogative and belonging" (T2, p. 280). *The Coming Insurrection* speaks derisively of existing forms of "organization" as a deadly matrix of separations, while calling for the birth of new "complicities," "sometimes ephemeral, but sometimes also unbetrayable" (TCI, p. 15). That split runs all the way through: on one side, an unrelenting attack on "the ensemble of dependencies" that cripple subjectivity; on the other, "a massive experimentation with new arrangements, new fidelities" (TCI, p. 42). The only way to resolve the problem is a kind of affective vanguardism: "We count on making that which is unconditional in relationships the armor of a political subjectivity as impenetrable to state interference as a gypsy camp." Here, in a single dramatic formulation, is the only permissible rule of organization: do not recognize any obligation that is not built on truth, trust, and love.

Is that enough? If so, we can move to the fourth moment and ask, Who will grow the carrots? This is not one of those flippant questions always raised by skeptics against Utopian schemes, pointing out that nobody will want to clean the toilets after the revolution. The text itself worries about growing carrots, which is to say, about the transition from a consistent political decision to actual material self-sufficiency. The introduction dismisses, with terrible scorn, the idea that "planting carrots is enough to dispel this nightmare" (TCI, p. 15), even while arguing in conclusion that "[acquiring] the skills to provide, over time, for one's own basic subsistence implies appropriating the necessary means of its production" (TCI, p. 125). Growing food takes time, and so does learning "to set bones and treat sicknesses," "understanding plankton biology and soil composition," and all those other tasks that must be learned, according to the text, in order to provide for communal living under the assumption of civil war (TCI, p. 107). But in order for each commune to be its own base, to constitute its own world, to speak its own language, the bonds must last. How is that to be done? It is hard to say: the text distrusts the impulse to decide any such thing in advance. In any case, even if an insurrection cannot begin with planting carrots, perhaps, if it succeeds, it will end there.

To recapitulate the larger argument we have been tracing: the possibility of a radical politics of indebtedness hinges on two attitudes or strategies that might at first appear opposed or contradictory, but actually refer to fundamentally different dimensions of the same situation. The first attitude, associated with microfinance, is based on the argument that human productivity itself requires indebtedness as a kind of irreducible technical prosthesis, and that far from dissolving this requirement, capitalism seizes it at every turn in order to submit it to the mechanisms of profit. In this respect, the condition of "indebtedness" will deepen to include various practical forms of relationality, encompassing all of the social circumstances and behaviors that allow us to speak of "associated workers" carrying out "socially necessary labor." In a capitalist setting, money comes to dominate all forms of relationality, so that people enable each other to be productive only through the mechanism of investments, loans, or some more complicated arrangement. As long as money sets the terms under which mutual assistance and cooperation take place, any Utopian vision that depends upon it will run into a series of familiar limitations, all of which come down to the fact that money turns the reciprocal dynamic of indebtedness into an inert and strictly material exchange.

The second attitude, associated with Jubilee, understands human capacities and powers in a more symbolic register, as forces that are capable of bringing justice to a corrupt system—or abolishing oppression by systems altogether. It insists that people must always be able to refuse the obligations built into their circumstances, and insofar as these obligations can be ruptured by an act of will (insofar, in other words, as they can be seen as merely symbolic), cancelling debts or going bankrupt is always somehow liberating. Not just once, but over and over: it becomes possible to believe that the process of liberation itself consists of stamping out every last obligation we might feel, even those we ourselves have made. There would be no point in arguing about any innate human capacity to be bound by a promise: no obligation can withstand the need to preserve or to restore one's capacity to live, that precious sense of self-reliance and autonomy.

Perhaps we cannot choose between these two attitudes. If the Utopia of microcredit imagines how economics might be conceived as universal mutual obligation, without transcendental rights or sacred duties, the Utopia of Jubilee imagines how economics as we know it can be jettisoned by an act of collective will. A politics of indebtedness thus poses a basic dialectical problem: how can the constructive and constitutive force of indebtedness be affirmed without erecting an appropriative and destructive apparatus? Does every debt that once might have appeared as a pivotal opening to the future always become the dead hand of the past? If debts somehow begin by expressing our own hopes, or even simply our own will to keep living, how is it that they so often end as precisely that which blocks us? The dialectic teaches that there is no going back, but that does not mean that there is always a way forward; the most we can say is that there is always a way out.

Let me illustrate the difficulty of this dialectic by turning to an apparently casual remark by Jean-Paul Sartre. In the middle of a 1970 conversation about happiness, he makes a blunt statement: "The goal of revolution is not to make everyone happy. It is to make everyone free and unalienated while dependent on each other."[9] The key formulation seems awkward. It begins straightforwardly: everyone should try to be free and unalienated. That's clear enough, although we really don't know how to go about it. What about the second part of the sentence, the part about depending on each other? How does that notion sit alongside the goal of freedom? Is Sartre saying that such dependence is merely a kind of background condition, or even an obstacle, to our pursuit of freedom? Or is he saying that being dependent on each other is *also* a goal, just as important as becoming free and unalienated? No doubt the sentence cannot help but follow

---

9   John Gerassi, ed. and trans., *Talking with Sartre: Conversations and Debates* (New Haven: Yale University Press, 2009), p. 28.

this syntax (the call of freedom first, then the recognition of dependence), because it would sound rather strange to say it the other way around, that the goal of revolution is to build our dependence on each other, while trying to be free. Yet that would be true, too.

Just as we must know how to compose bonds that make it possible to live together freely, we must also know how to break the bonds that deter us from living at all. And we are still learning who we are, this "we" that we owe it to ourselves to become.

Index